Skyhorse Publishing books may be purchased in bulk at special discounts for sales promotion, corporate gifts, fund-raising, or educational purposes. Special editions can also be created to specifications. For details, contact the Special Sales Department, Skyhorse Publishing, 307 West 36th Street, 11th Floor, New York, NY 10018 or info@skyhorsepublishing.com.

Skyhorse® and Skyhorse Publishing® are registered trademarks of Skyhorse Publishing, Inc.®, a Delaware corporation.

www.skyhorsepublishing.com

10 9 8 7 6 5 4 3 2 1

Library of Congress Cataloging-in-Publication Data is available on file.

ISBN: 978-1-62636-043-3

Printed in China

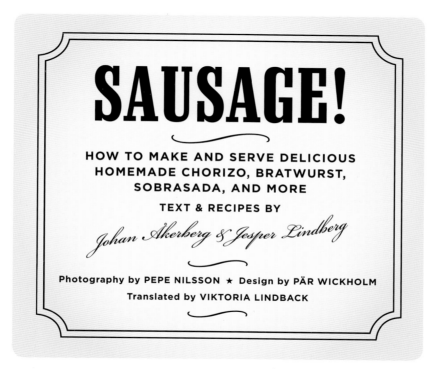

SAUSAGE!

HOW TO MAKE AND SERVE DELICIOUS
HOMEMADE CHORIZO, BRATWURST,
SOBRASADA, AND MORE

TEXT & RECIPES BY

Johan Åkerberg & Jesper Lindberg

Photography by PEPE NILSSON ★ Design by PÄR WICKHOLM
Translated by VIKTORIA LINDBACK

Skyhorse Publishing

— CONTENTS —

PREFACE

"Sausage was mentioned in the Odyssey and was a highly regarded dish in Ancient Rome. Apicius's Roman cookbook . . ."*

Hold up! Stop! This is not *that* type of cookbook. We promise we will refrain from delving into history, background, tradition, profundities, or famous quotes.

Instead, we will be writing about how FUN, SIMPLE, and WONDERFUL it is to craft homemade sausage!

Put simply, a sausage has two ends and can be prepared in numerous ways. This book is a journey toward the most delicious kinds of sausages and the best condiments. If you can make meatballs and hamburgers, you can make sausage. It is as simple as that.

You can choose between grinding your own meat or (if you'd prefer to make your life that little bit easier) purchasing ground meat at the grocery store.

And there are more options than just this! For example, choose between stuffing the sausage in traditional casings or leaving them as is. We'll show you recipes where the sausage has been rolled in plastic wrap and steamed, and those in which the sausage mixture is used as part of a pasta dish.

All right. You can drive yourself crazy delving into the contents of the Internet or literature on the subject. But this book is for anyone who wants to get started making delicious, simple, fun, wonderful, and flavorful sausage. We might not know best, but we know that we want to make sausage, because sausage is delicious!

Johan Åkerberg   Jesper Lindberg

*from the Swedish National Encyclopedia

THE RAW INGREDIENTS

Grind the meat or purchase it already ground. Really, you can use any type of meat, but it's important that the meat is not too lean, so pork is most commonly used. If you opt for a lean meat like game or poultry, you'll need to add extra fat.

If you're using store-bought ground meat, check to make sure it's not too lean. It ought to contain between 20–25% fat!

There are two types of sausages: The one that has been prepared and cooked ahead of time, and the one that remains raw until right before serving, when it is cooked, fried, or grilled. But you'll read more about this in the following recipes.

PORK

Pork is the ultimate meat for homemade sausage. It produces a juicy sausage, and the fat content is easy to control. As a result, pork is the main ingredient used in most sausages. Or it's added to recipes in which the predominant meat is too lean.

In some cultures, pork is combined with other meats or ingredients because of its delicious taste. For example, this can be seen in Asian dishes in which pork and seafood are combined.

Sausage is rarely made from the most exclusive of meat, because these just don't contain enough fat. Instead, sausage is made from ham, loin, shoulder, side, or stew meat. Smoked pork, bacon, and natural lard are also great because of their amazing taste. When it comes to delicious food, the pig is man's best friend. Even the Vikings agreed; according to Norse mythology, Odin's pig, Särimner, was slaughtered and eaten every night and resurrected in the morning. It was the ultimate joy in Valhalla!!! (Oops, we couldn't help but infuse some history. At least it was about a tasty pig . . .)

BEEF AND VEAL

If you're using beef or veal, you should go for cuts with the highest fat content. (Entrecôte is perfect, but let's just say that this would be a little over the top.)

If you're using nearly fat free meat, you should add some lard in order to make the sausage juicy.

Use beef loin, prime rib, side, shoulder, or stew beef. If you're purchasing ground meat instead, get a mix of approximately 80% beef and 20% pork.

GAME

Sausage made from game is mouthwateringly good, and it can be used in a wide variety of dishes and paired with some exciting condiments. Game is tasty and lean, so you'll have to add fat, such as cream, pork, or lard, to the mixture. This will make the sausage juicier than it would be otherwise.

Meat from our four-legged friends the moose, deer, boar, and rabbit might be a little tough—but the sausage is really delicious!

You can use any of the cuts that remain after the fillets and steaks have been put aside.

LAMB

Lamb has a relatively high fat content and is great for our purposes. Lamb steak, shank, and shoulder all provide a lot of flavor and make excellent sausage.

Lamb's characteristic flavor blends perfectly with the distinct, strong flavors of garlic, green spices, harissa (chili paste), and other strong chili spices.

POULTRY

You can use chicken, turkey, duck, or even ostrich. (Grouse that you've hunted yourself should probably be consumed in forms other than sausage!)

When it comes to sausage made from poultry, don't use the breast fillets—they're just too lean. Rather, go for the thigh fillets. And remember to use the skin when you grind the meat. If you're making turkey sausage, you should also use the wing meat. One exception is when you're making duck sausage; then you should use the breast. Just be sure to include the fat trimmings as well.

FISH

Go for fish with high fat content, such as salmon, herring, or cod. Pike is also good for binding the forcemeat.

When you are making fish sausage, think patée. In fact, you could say that you're actually making crab cakes in sausage form. For most fish sausages, you'll need something that binds the forcemeat, such as egg or cream, and this will also serve to make the sausage juicier.

Fish sausage can be stuffed in regular casings, but it can also be molded with plastic wrap before being steamed, or breaded and fried.

VEGETARIAN

When it comes to making vegetarian sausage, it's actually really simple: You can make sausage out of almost anything. Tofu, mushroom, corn, beans, bulgur, quorn, soy products . . . you'll just need to add egg or cream to bind the forcemeat.

This is also an opportunity to compose exciting and spicy flavor combinations. (However, if you're looking for flavor sensations and want to experience something extraordinary, we refer you to the pork section.)

MAKING HOMEMADE SAUSAGE

PREPARATION

There are two commandments when it comes to making sausage:
- Keep it clean!
- Keep it cool!

Wash your equipment carefully (cutting boards, knives, meat grinders, scales) with soap and hot water. Be mindful to wash your hands with soap and water continuously throughout the process.

It's important to keep the meat and other ingredients cool in order to minimize bacterial growth. (But, of course, it's perfectly fine to thaw the meat!)

Any meat that is to be ground should be cut into one inch squares. For the sake of cleaning up later, you might want to cut on a plastic cutting board that can be washed in a dishwasher.

Weigh the meat that is to be ground. Make sure to follow the recipe carefully, since the weight of the meat affects the amount of spices and other ingredients needed.

GRINDING THE MEAT

Most people use a stand mixer with a food grinder attachment, but you can also use a hand cranked meat grinder. These usually come with two grinding plates of different levels of coarseness. You can also chop the meat manually or buy ground meat at the store.

Some recipes recommend that the meat be ground twice. It will be easier and quicker the second time.

When the meat is ground, refrigerate. Remember—keep it cool!

SEASONING & MIXING

Measure the spices according to the recipe and combine in a bowl. The spices should be well mixed before they are added to the ground meat.

Pour cold water into the bowl of spices. This will ensure that the meat is kept cool and will make it easier to work with. The water will evaporate during the preparation process.

Mix the meat and the spices, either by hand or with a mixer with a dough hook attachment.

Once you've finished the sausage mix, it is time to taste the seasoning. Fry a piece of the forcemeat (the meat and spice mixture) and sample. Is the seasoning how you want it? Got enough salt? Modify if necessary, but keep in mind that the flavors will usually be more distinct in the finished sausage.

STUFFING THE SAUSAGE

There are many ways to stuff sausage. You can add an attachment to a kitchen appliance, a sausage stuffer attached to a hand-cranked meat grinder, a forcing bag, or you can even use the cut-off top of a plastic bottle. Or you can refrain from stuffing the sausage at all. If you're pressed for time and don't want to save, smoke, or dry the sausage, you can fry the meat as is. Grab a beer, make whatever condiments you want, and dig in!

But this book is about actually making sausage. And so here are some instructions on how to stuff sausage in casings. (Some sausages in this book remain unstuffed and are simply rolled in plastic wrap or fried directly.)

Casings are most commonly made from pig intestines, but they can also come from beef or lamb. If that makes you squeamish, there are also artificial casings made from collagen. Casings can be ordered from most deli counters at supermarkets.

Casings usually come in a box with a brine solution. Sometimes they are simply dry-salted. Remember, as the casings are being applied, the sausage stuffer must be kept wet. It's imperative that the casings be kept from drying.

Try to avoid air bubbles when cranking the grinder or when the machine is stuffing the meat into the casing. Maintain adequate resistance. Try it out a couple of times—it can be a bit difficult in the beginning but practice makes perfect.

When you're done, a long, curled sausage should appear in front of you. Twist the sausage or tie a string around the appropriate places so that the sausages become the desired size. Now it's time to fry, cook, dry in the oven, place in the freezer, or proudly hold up the sausage so that someone can snap a picture of the chef. This is a must for the family photo album or Facebook profile picture! And as for the rest: Follow the recipes!

Let the feast begin!

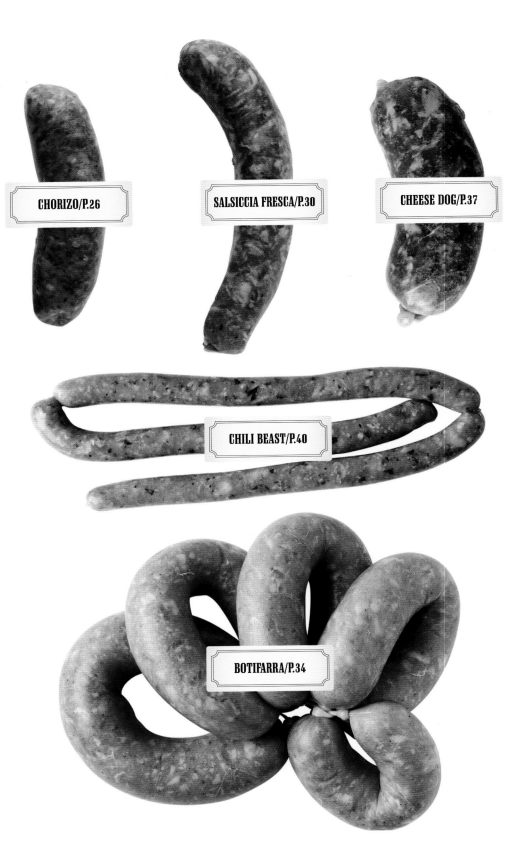

CHORIZO/P.26

SALSICCIA FRESCA/P.30

CHEESE DOG/P.37

CHILI BEAST/P.40

BOTIFARRA/P.34

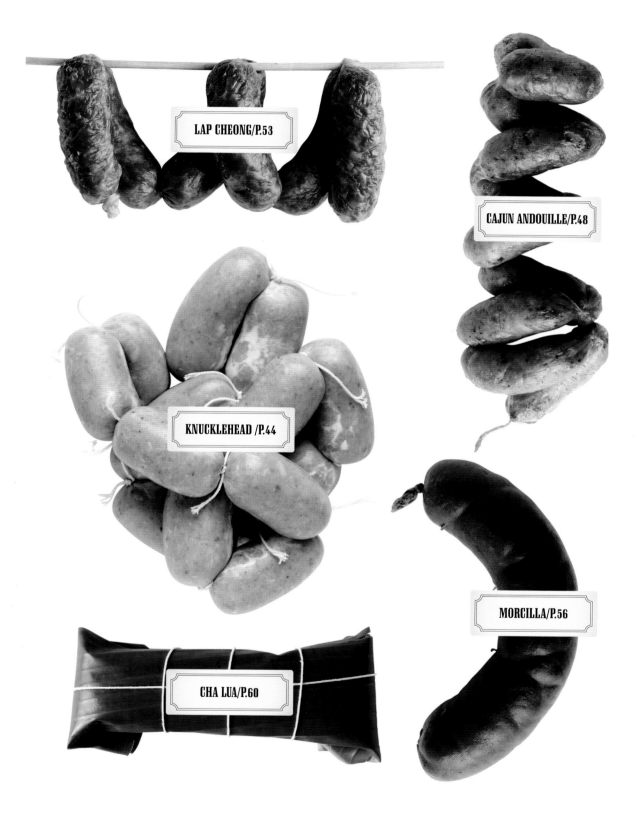

LAP CHEONG/P.53

CAJUN ANDOUILLE/P.48

KNUCKLEHEAD /P.44

MORCILLA/P.56

CHA LUA/P.60

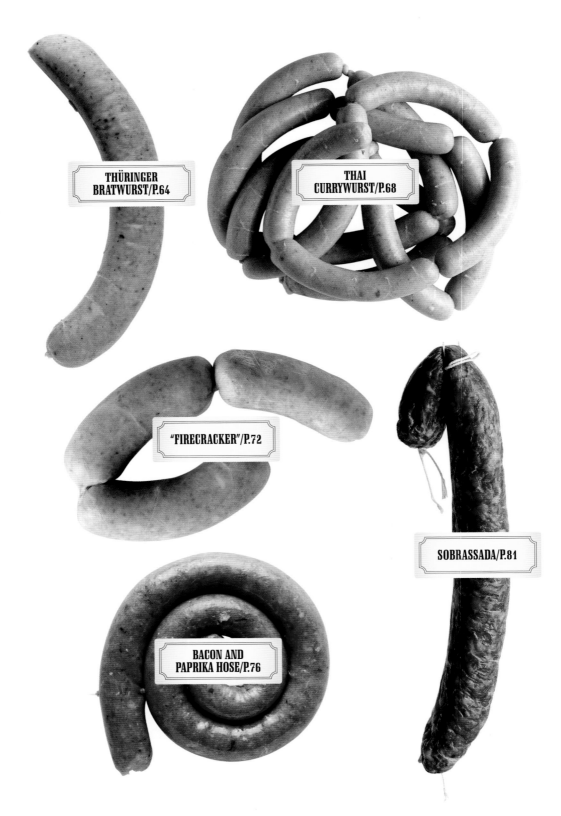

THÜRINGER BRATWURST/P.64

THAI CURRYWURST/P.68

"FIRECRACKER"/P.72

SOBRASSADA/P.81

BACON AND PAPRIKA HOSE/P.76

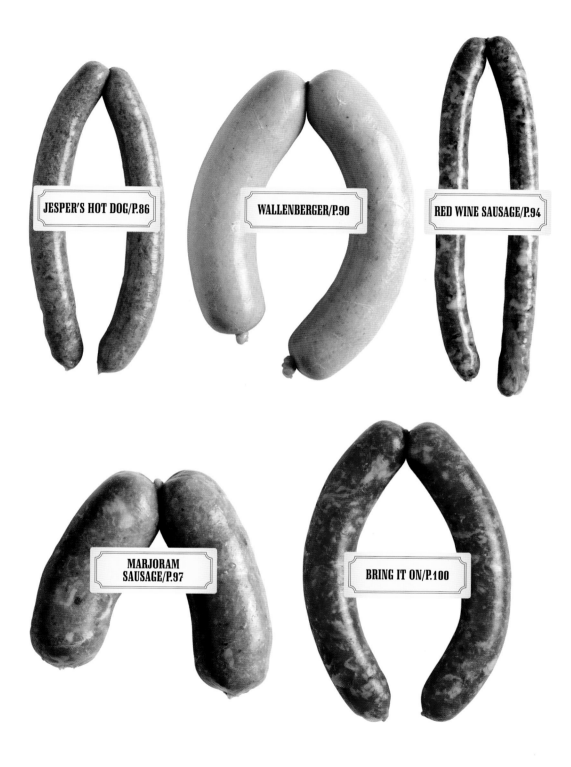

JESPER'S HOT DOG/P.86

WALLENBERGER/P.90

RED WINE SAUSAGE/P.94

MARJORAM
SAUSAGE/P.97

BRING IT ON/P.100

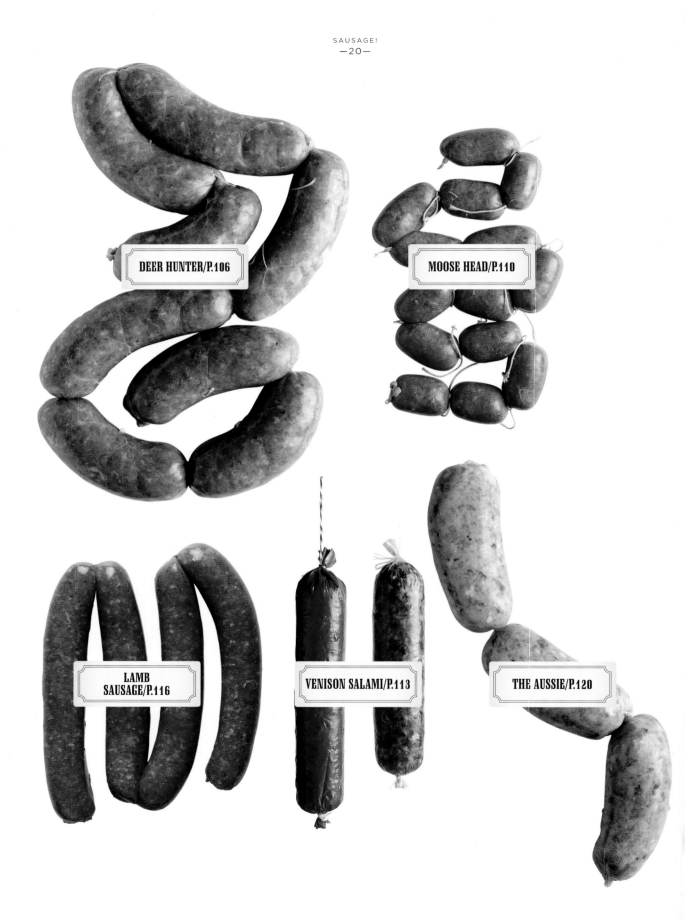

DEER HUNTER/P.106

MOOSE HEAD/P.110

LAMB
SAUSAGE/P.116

VENISON SALAMI/P.113

THE AUSSIE/P.120

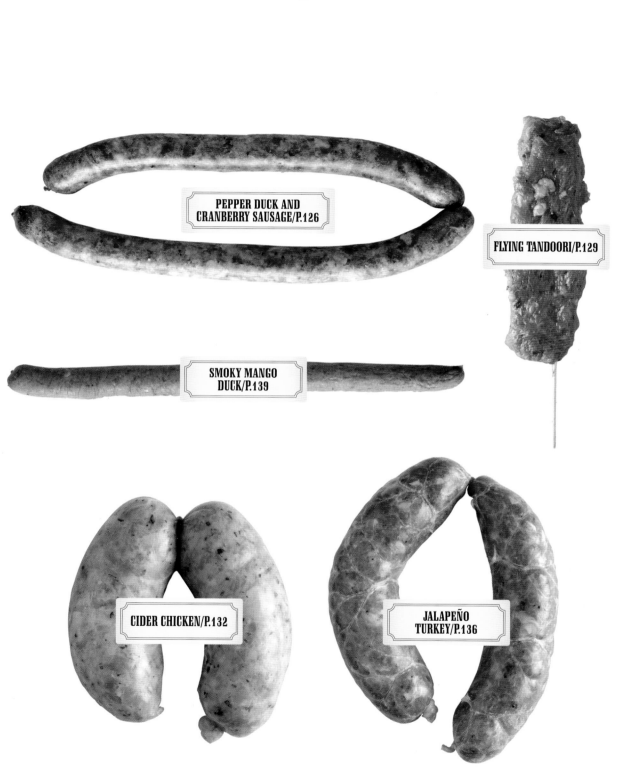

PEPPER DUCK AND
CRANBERRY SAUSAGE/P.126

FLYING TANDOORI/P.129

SMOKY MANGO
DUCK/P.139

CIDER CHICKEN/P.132

JALAPEÑO
TURKEY/P.136

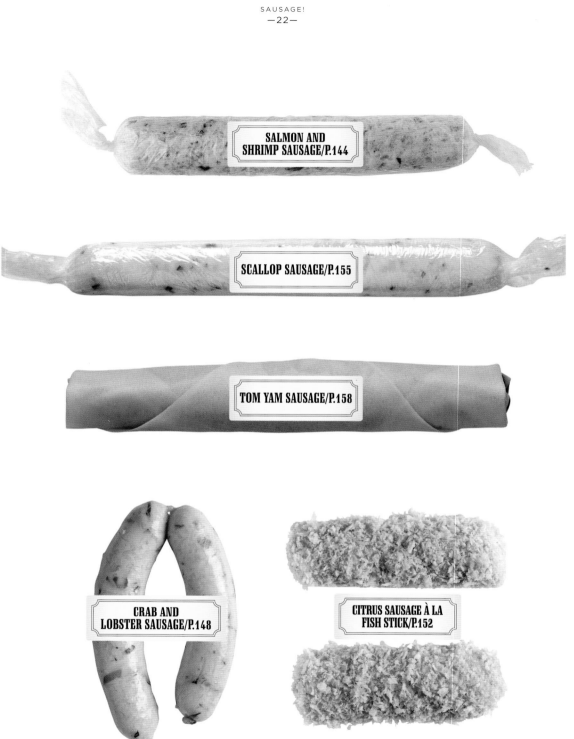

SALMON AND
SHRIMP SAUSAGE/P.144

SCALLOP SAUSAGE/P.155

TOM YAM SAUSAGE/P.158

CRAB AND
LOBSTER SAUSAGE/P.148

CITRUS SAUSAGE À LA
FISH STICK/P.152

SMOKY BEAN SAUSAGE/P.164

MUSHROOM AND
RICE SAUSAGE/P.167

ZUCCHINI AND MOZZARELLA
ROLL/P.176

CHICKPEA AND
CHILI WURST/P.170

SPICY TOFU
ROLL/P.173

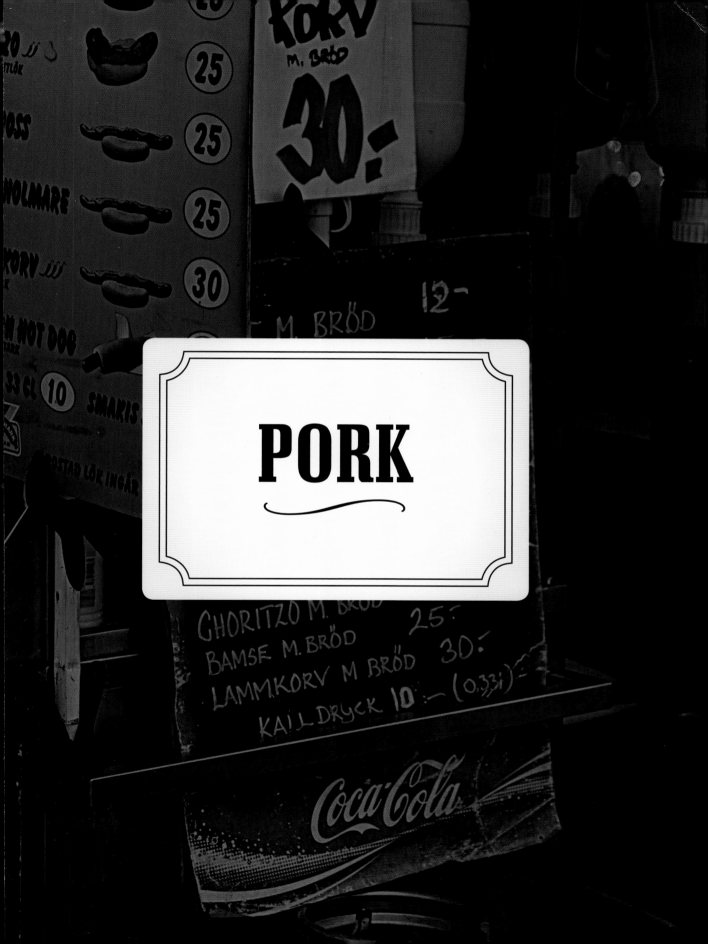

PORK

BARBECUE SANDWICH WITH A KICK

CHORIZO IN A BUN WITH SALSA AND GRATED CHEESE

CHORIZO HAS BECOME A favorite among many. It's rich in flavor and is a little bit on the spicy side. When you make it yourself you can get the right amount of "kick" for your taste buds. Once you've tasted your own home-made chorizo, forget the hot dog stand's diluted sausages and the super-market's plastic bags with their supposedly "protective atmosphere!" With its chili flavors and Spanish paprika (this can be purchased at a properly varied spice store), this chorizo will be spicy!

(Approx. 7–9 sausages)
1 ⅔ lbs (750 g) pork tenderloin, diced
½ lb (250 g) chuck roll, diced
2 garlic cloves
2 tsp Pimentón de La Vera, Picante (smoky and spicy paprika)
½ tbsp chili flakes
½ tsp ground nutmeg
1 tbsp non-iodized salt
½ cup (100 ml) red wine, ice-cold

Grind the meat and the garlic on the medium setting.

Combine the forcemeat with the spices and red wine. Mix for approximately 10 minutes.

Fry a piece of the meat and sample. Adjust seasoning to taste.

Stuff the meat in pork casings and make sausages that are between 3–4 inches (8–10 cm) long.

Hang dry for 1–2 hours before placing in the refrigerator.

Ideally, you should let the sausages sit for 24 hours so the flavors have ample time to develop.

Fry or grill before serving.

SERVING

Split the sausage lengthwise and fry or grill it. Place the sausage immediately in a sourdough bun and sprinkle with hot salsa and grated cheese (manchego is best, but parmesan works well too).

QUICK SALSA

3 vine tomatoes, diced
½ cucumber, cored and diced
1 red onion, chopped
1–2 chili peppers, thinly sliced
1 bundle of cilantro, chopped
3 ½ tbsp oil
2–3 tbsp white wine vinegar
1 tbsp unrefined sugar
salt and pepper

Mix all of the ingredients and add vinegar, salt, and pepper to taste. Let the salsa sit in the refrigerator so the flavors have time to develop.

WONDERFULLY SIMPLE PASTA

SALSICCIA FRESCA WITH TOMATO SAUCE AND PASTA

"IF YOU'RE NOT ITALIAN, fake it!" We're recreating authentic Italian passion for food in this spicy and flavorful dish that pairs salsiccia sausage with pasta and tomato sauce.

For this dish, you'll have to cut the sausage open to use its contents. (To make it easy on yourself, you can create the dish directly from the sausage mixture. But why do things have to be easy? Maybe because you're in a rush to go to Italy . . .?) This type of salsiccia is fresh and seasoned with fennel and salvia. The salted pork adds flavor and saltiness, but it can be switched out according to taste. Grated cheese helps the flavors mature even more.

(Approx. 10–12 sausages)
2 lbs (1 kg) pork tenderloin, diced
¾ lb (300 g) salted pork, diced
⅔ cup (150 ml) grated pecorino or parmesan cheese
2 tbsp crushed fennel seeds
1 tsp dried sage
½ tsp ground nutmeg
1 tsp chili flakes
1 tsp non-iodized salt
2 tsp coarse black pepper
⅔ cup (150 ml) red wine, ice-cold

Grind the meat on the coarsest setting.

Add cheese, spices, and red wine to the meat and mix for about 5 minutes.

Refrigerate in the bowl for 3–4 hours.

Fry a piece of the meat and sample. Adjust seasoning to taste.

Stuff the meat in pork casings and make sausages that are approximately 8–10 inches (15–20 cm) in length.

Hang dry for 1–2 hours before refrigerating.

Let the sausages sit for 24 hours before serving so the flavors have ample time to develop.

Fry or grill before serving.

SERVING

Split the sausages and fry in a pan while the pasta is boiling. Into the pan with the sausage, add some white wine, a quality tomato sauce, some fresh sage leaves, butter, and other delicious things. When the pasta's ready, stir it all together and add the grated cheese. Enjoy with any bottle of Italian red wine!

SALSICCIA PASTA WITH MARINARA SAUCE

2 salsiccia sausages
½ onion, finely chopped
½–1 red chili pepper, thinly sliced
½ cup (100 ml) white wine
¾–1 ¼ cups (200–300 ml) quality
    tomato sauce

2 tbsp butter
10 basil leaves
salt and pepper
freshly grated parmesan
4 servings of pasta, preferably
    penne

Split the sausages and squeeze out the contents in a hot pan. Brown the meat. Add the onion and chili pepper and fry for a few more minutes.

Add the white wine and tomato sauce. Let it simmer and add the butter and basil leaves. Season with salt and pepper to taste.

When the pasta's ready, drain the water and add the sauce. Top with a little bit of parmesan.

Let the sauce mix with the pasta, then serve topped with more parmesan and freshly ground black pepper.

(Save some of the water from the cooked pasta to dilute the sauce if it's too dry. There's a lot of flavor in that water).

TOMATO SAUCE

2 tbsp olive oil
½ onion, chopped
1 garlic clove, chopped
2 cans of whole tomatoes
3–4 basil leaves
½ tbsp sugar

Heat the oil in a pot and sweat the
onion and garlic until soft.
Add tomatoes, basil, and sugar.
Boil and then let simmer for 45–60
minutes. Stir occasionally.
Remove from the stove and strain
until the sauce is smooth.
Store the sauce in a cool place until
ready to serve.

SIMPLY A DELICIOUS SANDWICH!

BOTIFARRA IN A BUN WITH COARSE-GRAINED MUSTARD AND BROCCOLI

JUST TASTE THE NAME!! It can't be anything but delicious! Botifarra hails primarily from Catalonia in northern Spain but it can also be found in Mallorca and in parts of North Africa. "Botifarra" means sausage, and it comes in a variety of types. It's precooked before being prepared. Pimentón de la Vera is a smoky, Spanish paprika. Picante = hot, dulce = sweet. Try to get your hands on it; if you can't, well then just use regular paprika. It will come out just as tasty!

(Approx. 4–5 sausages)
1 ½ lbs (700 g) pork shoulder, diced
⅔ lb (300 g) lard, diced
2 cloves, ground in a mortar
½ tsp ground cinnamon
¼ tsp Pimentón de la Vera, Picante
1 tsp Pimentón de la Vera, Dulce
1 tbsp non-iodized salt
3 ½ tbsp (50 ml) dry white wine, ice-cold

Grind the meat and lard on the coarsest setting.

Mix the meat with the spices and white wine for about 10–15 minutes.

Fry a piece of the meat and sample the seasoning. Adjust to taste.

Stuff the meat in pork casings and form sausages that are 14–16 inches (35–40 cm) long. Tie both ends together to emulate the shape of a horseshoe.

Place the sausage in water 158°F (70°C) for 30 minutes. Be careful: The sausage should NEVER boil!

Rinse the sausages in cold water until they reach a temperature of roughly 59°F (15°C).

Let the sausage sit for 24 hours before serving so the flavors have ample time to develop.

Store in the refrigerator, wrapped in paper.

SERVING

The following condiments are simple and delicious and will also work well with the salsiccia sausage. The trick is to fry the sausages in a bit of butter and set them aside. Then fry both the bread and the broccoli in the same pan. Finally, just add some coarse-grained mustard!

COARSE-GRAINED MUSTARD

1 bag yellow mustard seeds
1 bag brown mustard seeds
3 tbsp water
1 tsp white vinegar
½ tsp salt
Cognac for flavor!

Pour half of the yellow and brown mustard seeds in a mixer. Add the water.

Mix until it becomes a paste.

Use a mortar to crush the rest of the seeds. Then mix with the paste and add vinegar, salt, and cognac to taste.

SAY CHEESE!

CHEESE DOG IN A BAGUETTE WITH CHEESE SAUCE

CHEESE DOGS! CAN IT get any better? Johan first encountered the cheese dog on a trip to the United States. It's fairly hot and spicy, which balances well with the two types of cheese. Feel free to choose between different cheeses, such as blue cheese or a nice gruyère.

(Approx. 12–14 sausages)
2 lbs (1 kg) pork, diced
½ tbsp fennel seeds
1 bay leaf
⅔ cup (150 ml) grated parmesan
⅔ cup (150 ml) shredded mozzarella
1½ tbsp finely chopped parsley
3 garlic cloves, pressed
½ tsp chili flakes
2 tsp non-iodized salt
½ tsp fresh, coarse black pepper
½ cup (100 ml) dry red wine, ice cold

Grind the meat, fennel seeds, and bay leaf on the finest setting.

Mix the forcemeat with the rest of the spices and the red wine for about 10 minutes.

Fry a piece of the meat and sample. Adjust seasoning to taste.

Stuff the meat in pork casings and make sausages that are about 4 inches (10 cm) long.

Hang dry for about 1–2 hours before refrigerating.

Ideally, you should let the sausages sit for 24 hours before serving so that the flavors have ample time to develop.

Fry or grill before serving!

SERVING

Cheese needs cheese! We have friends who would die for some tasty, melted cheese, so here's even more to go on top of the sausages. Serve in a delicious bun.

CHEESE SAUCE

¾ cup (200 ml) cream
¾ cup (200 ml) white wine
4 slices American cheddar
1 ¼ cups (300 ml) grated mozzarella
¾ cup (200 ml) grated parmesan
½ tsp cayenne pepper

Place all ingredients in a pot and heat over a medium flame while stirring. Pour over the cheese dog!

CHILI ALL IN!

A CHILI BEAST IN A BAGUETTE WITH CHEDDAR CHEESE, TEXAS CHILI, SOUR CREAM, PICKLED CHILIES, MOZZARELLA, AND DEEP-FRIED ONIONS.

PORK WORKS WELL WITH almost anything—especially if you're yearning for some extra heat. If you let the sausage sit overnight, the "kick" will be even more distinct.

This is an American monster with a lot of flavor! And it's a lot to eat. Extra everything!

Leftovers are guaranteed, so plan on an additional meal. Make sure the tequila and beer are ice-cold!

(Approx. 23–25 sausages)
1 ¾ lbs (800 g) pork, diced
⅔ lb (300 g) lard, diced
⅔ cup (150 ml) grated pecorino
1 red onion, coarsely grated
2 jalapeños, finely chopped
1 red chili pepper, finely chopped

5 garlic cloves, pressed
1 tbsp liquid smoke
2 tsp chili flakes
1 ½ tbsp paprika
2 tsp non-iodized salt
1 ½ tbsp coarse black pepper
⅔ cup (150 ml) pilsner or pale lager, ice-cold

Grind the meat and the lard on the coarsest setting.

Mix the forcemeat with the cheese, spices, and the beer for about 10 minutes. Fry a piece of the meat and sample.

Stuff the meat in sheep casing and make sausages that are about 8 inches (20 cm) long.

Hang dry for approximately 1–2 hours before refrigerating.

Let the sausages sit for 24 hours before serving so the flavors have ample time to develop.

Fry or grill when your next chili craving comes by!

SERVING

Split the baguette and top with a couple of slices of cheddar. Heat in the oven until the cheese is melted and add the grilled sausage. Top with Texas chili, pickled chili peppers, mozzarella cheese, sour cream, and fried onions. Finger-licking good! Go Texas!!

TEXAS CHILI

2 lbs (1 kg) chuck roll, diced
1 onion, chopped
3 garlic cloves, chopped
1 tbsp ground ancho chili
2 chili peppers, sliced
3 Thai chilies, sliced
½ tbsp chili powder

½ tbsp chili flakes
2 tbsp paprika
½ tbsp cumin
1 tbsp oregano
1 can whole tomatoes
1 can light beer
salt and pepper

Brown the chuck roll in a pan with oil and place it in a separate pot. In the same pan as the one used to brown the meat, brown the onion and the garlic and add the chili. Stir this mixture into the meat. Add the paprika, cumin, oregano, and tomatoes and cover with beer. Bring to a boil and simmer with the lid on for 2–3 hours. The meat should be so tender that it collapses when touched. Remove the lid and let simmer until it reaches the desired texture. Add salt and pepper to taste.

PICKLED CHILIES

½ cup (100 ml) vinegar
½ cup (100 ml) sugar
¾ cup (200 ml) water
10 red chili peppers, sliced
½ inch ginger, sliced

Mix the vinegar, sugar, and water and stir
until the sugar has dissolved.
Add the chili and the ginger and let sit in
the refrigerator before serving.

DEEP-FRIED ONIONS

3 peeled onions
4 ¼ cups (1 liter) deep-frying oil
salt

Slice the onions into thin rings and put in a
bowl with ice-cold water. Separate the rings
and let sit for 30 minutes.
Drain the water and dry the rings thoroughly with paper towels or a cloth.
Heat the oil to 320–340°F(160–170°C).
Test a few of the onion rings to see if the oil
is hot enough. Fry the onions in batches and
stir occasionally so that they become evenly
brown.
Remove the onion rings and drain on a
paper towel.
Salt and serve.
Store any leftovers in an airtight container.

KNUCKLEHEAD

HAM HOCK SAUSAGE WITH MASHED POTATOES, PICKLED ROOT VEGETABLES, AND HOT HONEY MUSTARD

WE LOVE HAM HOCK in all forms! Cooked, roasted, pulled, salted, unsalted, etc. This recipe reinvents the old classic into a sausage made from salted ham hock and spiced with a specific mixture. These make small sausages! They go well with the condiments.

(Approx. 22–24 sausages)
1 ⅔ lbs (750 g) brined ham hock, deboned
½ lb (250 g) fat from the meat, or lard
1 garlic clove
10 allspice corns
2 bay leaves
½ tbsp ground ginger
½ tsp non-iodized salt
1 tbsp black pepper
¾ cup (200 ml) pilsner or pale lager, ice cold

Grind the meat, lard, garlic, allspice corns, and bay leaves on the finest setting and place in a blender.

Add salt, ginger, black pepper, and beer and blend for about 5 minutes.

Fry a piece of the forcemeat and sample the seasoning.

Stuff the meat in pork casings and form sausages that are about 2 inches (5 cm) long. Tie with twine.

Hang dry for 1–2 hours before refrigerating.

Let the sausage sit for 24 hours before serving so the flavors have ample time to develop. Poach the sausages in the sausage stock before serving.

SERVING

Serve with flavors that pair well with the sausage, such as homemade mashed potatoes with pickled turnips and carrots, and of course, delicious hot mustard.

SAUSAGE STOCK

8 ½ cups (2 liters) water
1 ¼ cups (300 ml) light beer
2 bay leaves
10 white peppercorns
1 carrot, peeled and sliced
1 red onion, halved
1 stalk of celery, sliced
2 tbsp salt

Bring all the ingredients to a boil and let simmer for 10 minutes before removing from the stove. Let sit overnight before re-heating. Add the sausages and simmer until ready to serve. (Of course, if you're too hungry to wait, you can also skip this step and heat the sausage directly!)

PICKLED ROOT VEGETABLES

1 lb (500 g) grated root vegetables
    (e.g. carrots, parsnip, celeriac, turnip)
⅓ of a leek, thinly sliced
⅔ cup (150 ml) white vinegar
⅔ cup (150 ml) sugar
1 ⅓ cups (300 ml) water

Mix the vinegar, sugar, and water until the sugar has dissolved.
Add the grated root vegetables and the leek.
Stir and let sit for an hour before serving.
For stronger flavor, let sit overnight.

MASHED POTATOES

2 lbs (1 kg) peeled potatoes
½ cup (100 ml) milk
½ cup (100 ml) heavy cream
3 ½ tbsp (50 g) butter
1–2 tbsp sugar
salt and white pepper

Cook the potatoes in lightly salted water. Drain the water and let the potatoes steam. Heat the milk, cream, and butter. Run the potatoes through a potato press or use a potato masher. Mix the mashed potatoes with the milk, cream, and butter mixture. Mix until the mashed potatoes become porous and add salt and pepper to taste.

HOT HONEY MUSTARD

½ cup (100 ml) Colman's Mustard Powder
⅓ cup (75 ml) hot water
5 tsp (25 ml) honey
salt and white pepper

Mix the mustard powder and water in a bowl until it is smooth. Add the honey and let sit for 10–15 minutes. Add more honey, salt, and pepper to taste.

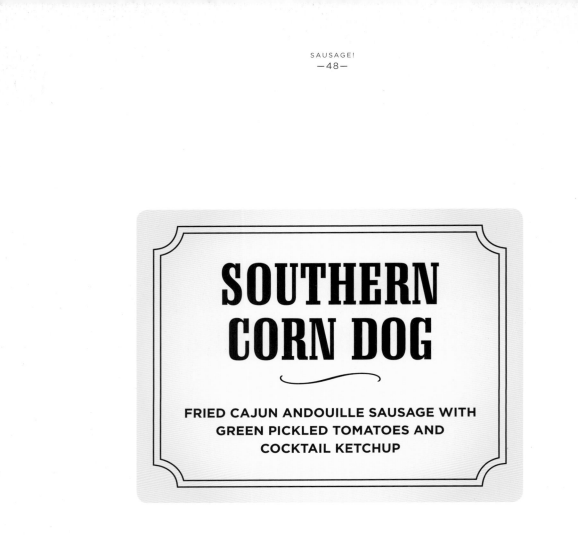

SOUTHERN CORN DOG

FRIED CAJUN ANDOUILLE SAUSAGE WITH GREEN PICKLED TOMATOES AND COCKTAIL KETCHUP

THIS IS A SAUSAGE from the American South and it is supposed to be smoked for about 7–8 hours in 150–175°F (70–75°C) smoke. We, however, will be using liquid smoke instead. Dry the sausage in the oven according to the recipe. If you don't want your sausages to wrinkle, it's essential that you cool them immediately after smoking.

(Approx. 14–16 sausages)
2 lbs (1 kg) pork tenderloin, diced
½ lb (250 g) lard
6 garlic cloves
1 tsp dried thyme
1 ½ tbsp chili flakes
2 tbsp paprika
2 tsp non-iodized salt
1 tbsp coarse black pepper
1 tbsp liquid smoke
⅔ cup (150 ml) ice water

Grind the meat, lard, and garlic on the coarsest setting.

Mix the forcemeat with the spices and ice water for about 10 minutes.

Fry a piece of the meat and sample.

Stuff in pork casing and make sausages that are about 4 inches (10 cm) long.

Pierce the sausages on sticks and dry in the oven at 175°F (75°C) for about 7–8 hours.

Remove the sausages from the oven and place them immediately in cold water. Let them soak until they reach a temperature of about 60°F (15°C). Remove the sausages from the water and let them dry before refrigerating.

Fry, grill, or make corn dogs!

SERVING

After seeing "corn dogs" in movies and hearing about them, Johan decided that it was time to try them himself. Usually you can make corn dogs from regular hot dogs, but it's certainly more fun to make a thicker and more flavorful sausage from scratch.

Make sure that the frying batter is not too thick and that it covers the whole sausage.

Fry a couple of sausages at a time so they don't stick to one another. Serve with a classic condiment (like pickled green tomatoes) or with a more modern interpretation (cocktail ketchup with vanilla!).

CORN DOG BATTER

1 cup (250 ml) flour
¾ cup (200 ml) cornmeal
2 tbsp polenta
3 tbsp sugar
1 tsp salt
2 tsp baking powder
1 cup (250 ml) milk
¼ cup (50 ml) water
1 egg
deep-frying oil

Mix the dry ingredients and the milk, water, and egg in two separate bowls. Heat the oil to 320–340°F (160–170°C).

Add the milk mixture to the bowl with the dry ingredients and let it sit for 10 minutes.

Fill a tall glass with the mixture (don't use all of it in one go!). Pierce each sausage with a stick, roll them in flour, shake off any excess, and dip each sausage in the glass. The batter should cover the entire sausage. Add more mixture to the glass as you go.

Once the sausage is coated in batter, place the sausage in the hot oil.

Fry the corn dogs for 5–6 minutes until they are golden brown. Make sure they are evenly fried.

Remove them from the oil and drain on paper towels before serving.

COCKTAIL KETCHUP WITH VANILLA

1 lb (500 g) cherry tomatoes
¾ cup (200 ml) sugar
⅔ cup (150 ml) white wine vinegar
1 tsp Korean chili flakes
2 tbsp tomato paste
1 vanilla bean, split
½ tsp ground ginger
salt

Place all ingredients in a saucepan. Boil with the lid on and let simmer for 2 hours. Stir occasionally until the ketchup reaches the desired consistency. Flavor with salt when the ketchup is ready.

THE RECIPE CONTINUES ON THE NEXT PAGE.

PICKLED GREEN TOMATOES

3 ⅓ lbs (1 ½ kg) tomatoes, preferably small, firm, and green
8 ½ cups (2 liters) water
1 tbsp salt
1 ¾ cup (400 ml) white vinegar

2 ½ cups (600 ml) water
2 cups + 2 tbsp (500 ml) sugar
3 slices of ginger
5 cloves
10 white peppercorns

Rinse the tomatoes, remove any remnants of the stem, and make small
holes in the tomato skin with a toothpick or knife tip.

Heat the water along with 1 tablespoon of salt in a pot. Add the tomatoes
and let them simmer for a maximum of 2 minutes. Remove the tomatoes
and rinse in a colander.

Sterilize the cans in which you will be storing the pickled tomatoes by
heating them in the oven for 10 minutes at 250°F (120°C), or boil them for
the same amount of time.

In the meantime, cook the vinegar, water, sugar, ginger, cloves, and white
peppercorns until the sugar dissolves. Simmer the tomatoes in the
"preserving juice" for 10 minutes.

Remove the tomatoes and place in jars.

Bring the "preserving juice" to a boil and pour into the jars, covering the
tomatoes completely.

Immediately put the lids on the jars and cool. Store in a dark and cool
place until serving.

SOUP DU JOUR

SOUP WITH LAP CHEONG, BOK CHOY, AND DRIED SHRIMP

THIS DRIED PORK SAUSAGE derives from southern China. You can buy it in most Asian grocery stores and it's delicious. You should try making it yourself! A hallelujah moment awaits . . .

It's important for the sausage's shelf life that it be dried properly, but you should also fry a piece before drying it. It's really tasty that way too! The wine, the whisky, and the five spice powder provides a very distinct flavor that makes the lap cheong irresistible. It's great for both hot and cold dishes.

(Approx. 16–18 sausages)
2 lbs (1 kg) pork tenderloin, diced
½ lb (250 g) lard, diced
1 tsp five spice powder
3 tbsp brown sugar
2 tbsp Chinese soy sauce
1 tbsp Chinese cooking wine or sweet sherry
2 tbsp whisky
2 tsp non-iodized salt
½ cup (100 ml) ice water

Grind the meat and lard on the coarsest setting.

Mix the forcemeat thoroughly with the spices, sugar, soy, wine, whisky, and ice water for about 5–10 minutes.

Fry a piece of the meat and sample.

Stuff the meat in pork casings and make sausages that are about 4 ½–5 ½ inches (12–14 cm) long.

Let the sausages sit in the refrigerator overnight. Keep them in a bowl covered with foil.

Heat the oven to 167°F (75°C). "Impale" the sausages on sticks and place them in the oven. Make sure they don't touch each other. Dry them for about 5–6 hours.

Remove the sausages from the oven and place in cold water until they reach a temperature of 60°F (15°C).

Remove from the water and let dry before storing them in the refrigerator.

SERVING

This lap cheong is served in a nice broth (preferably use chicken stock, but beef stock works too) like a delicious Chinese soup. Use vegetables such as bok choy or scallions and some shrimp. Add rice vinegar and freshly ground white pepper for a lovely combination of flavors. (This tip comes from Chef Ming, a highly skilled chef at Formosa, a great Chinese restaurant in Stockholm.)

SOUP STOCK

4 ¼ cups (1 liter) water
2 tbsp chicken broth
2 star anises
2 garlic cloves, crushed
1 onion, chopped
2 slices of ginger
½ stalk lemongrass
2–3 tbsp rice vinegar
2–3 tbsp fish sauce
black pepper

Bring the water to a boil and add the broth, star anises, garlic, onion, ginger, and lemongrass.

Let simmer for 15 minutes and strain into a saucepan. Add rice vinegar, fish sauce, and black pepper to taste.

BLOOD SAUSAGE IN MADRID

DEEP-FRIED MORCILLA WITH HUSH PUPPIES AND CHILI KETCHUP

SAUSAGE THAT USES BLOOD as an ingredient exists in many countries in a variety shapes and forms. Sweden, for instance, has blood pudding. This sausage contains some of that traditional taste as well as some Spanish influences.

Make sure the batter is firm enough to be stuffed into casings.

You should strive to let the sausage simmer in a stock before frying or deep-frying. It's also delicious to serve freshly cooked.

(Approx. 6–8 sausages)
2 onions, finely chopped
2 tbsp butter
½ cup (100 ml) raisins
1 tsp ground ginger
1 ⅓ lbs (600 g) fresh pork belly or tenderloin
⅔ cup (150 ml) heavy cream
3 slices white bread with crust removed
½ cup (100 ml) finely chopped parsley
1 bay leaf
½ tsp thyme
1 ½ tsp non-iodized salt
½ tsp freshly ground white pepper
2 cups + 2 tbsp (500 ml) ice-cold pig blood (this can be ordered at the deli counter)

Heat the pan with butter and fry the onions until they become golden in color. Add the raisins and ginger and let the mixture cool.

Grind the meat on the coarsest setting.

Mix the cream, bread, and spices in a bowl and let the bread rise for about 5 minutes.

Combine the cream mixture, onion mixture, blood, and forcemeat for about 10 minutes. (Feel free to add more bread if the mixture is too loose.)

Loosely stuff the batter in pork casings and make sausages that are about 6–8 inches (15–20 cm) long.

Place the sausages in a saucepan with cold water and heat to about 175–190°F (80–90°C). Maintain that temperature for 20–30 minutes and make sure that the temperature of the sausages reaches 160°F (70°C).

Test the sausages by poking them with a fork. If liquid comes out clear, the sausages are ready.

Remove the sausages and quickly rinse in cold water until they reach a temperature of 60°F (15°C).

Let dry before refrigerating.

Fry whole or sliced, or deep-fry them the Spanish way.

SERVING

A friend who just visited Madrid said that she had eaten breakfasts of deep-fried morcilla for a week, and she thought the sausage was simply delicious. This is what inspired this recipe. Here we will serve the morcilla sausage with tiny, deep fried hush puppies, and of course, some chili ketchup to balance the sweet and sour flavors.

HUSH PUPPIES

2 cups (500 ml) cornmeal
1 cup (250 ml) flour
1 tbsp salt
4 tsp baking powder
1 cup (250 ml) half-and-half
⅓ cup (75 g) melted butter
1 tsp Tabasco
2 onions, finely chopped
oil for deep-frying

Mix the flour, salt, and baking powder in a bowl.
In a separate bowl, mix the cream, butter, Tabasco, and onion.
In a pan, heat the oil to a temperature of 340–355°F (170–180°C).
Add the cream mixture and the dry ingredients and let sit for 10 minutes.
Fill a piping bag with the batter and pipe out dollops that measure 3–4 inches (8–10 cm) long. Fry them for 1–2 minutes until they turn golden in color.
Remove and let sit on a paper towel before serving.

CHILI KETCHUP

½ cup (100 ml) Sriracha sauce
½ cup (100 ml) ketchup
1 tsp Tabasco
2 tbsp sugar
2 tbsp white wine vinegar
salt and pepper

Mix all ingredients.
Sample with salt, pepper, and possibly some sugar and vinegar to attain the right balance of flavors.

BANH MI TOTAL

CHA LUA SAUSAGE IN A BAGUETTE
WITH PICKLED ROOT VEGETABLES,
CHICKEN LIVER MOUSSE, MAYONNAISE,
CILANTRO, JALAPEÑO CHILI,
NUOC CHAM SAUCE, AND CUCUMBER

JOHAN HAD THIS VIETNAMESE sausage on this particular sandwich for breakfast in Hanoi a couple of years ago. Cha lua is reminiscent of bologna but without the smoky flavor. Here the sausage is eaten cold, but it also works well if you fry it in thick slices.

Remember that the baking powder makes the sausage rise slightly, so don't stuff it too tightly. If you don't have access to banana leaves, you can use plastic foil.

(Approx. 4–6 sausages)
2 lbs (1 kg) pork tenderloin, diced
2 tbsp fish sauce
1 tbsp sugar
1 cup (250 ml) ice water
2 tbsp tapioca flour (available in Asian grocery stores)
1 tbsp baking powder
banana leaves or plastic wrap
twine

Grind the meat on the finest setting 2–3 times.

Mix the forcemeat with the fish sauce and sugar.

In a separate bowl, combine the ice water, tapioca flour, and baking powder. Let it foam.

Add the liquid to the meat mixture and store covered with foil in a cold place for about 6 hours.

Mix the forcemeat in a mixer for 5–10 minutes.

Distribute the meat onto 4–6 banana leaves (or sheets of plastic wrap).
Roll, fold in the edges, and tie them together with twine.

Steam the sausages at 195–210°F (90–100°C) for 20–30 minutes. Keep in
mind that the baking powder will cause them to expand a bit. (Steam
them in a colander over a saucepan of hot water that has been placed
beneath the oven rack.)

Let the rolls cool before refrigerating.

Before serving, unwrap the banana leaf/plastic wrap and fry the contents
or serve cold in a sandwich.

SERVING

The Vietnamese super sandwich Banh Mi has spread quickly to all corners
of the world—including the hottest restaurants and food joints in New
York City. This is completely understandable—this sandwich has it all!
As for spreads and condiments, there is an endless variety that go with
this sandwich. The most important part is the bread: it should have a
crispy exterior and a fluffy interior so that you can really load it up.
The sandwich should contain nuoc cham (a Vietnamese dipping sauce),
cucumber, and cilantro. Besides that, you can pretty much add anything
you want—a fried egg, for example.

Johan is very enthusiastic about Banh Mi: "I went berserk and filled it with
numerous things, such as nuoc cham, mayonnaise, soy, pickles, cucumber,
cilantro, red onion, chicken liver mousse, jalapeños, and of course, some
cha lua."

Start with the sliced sausage and load it up!

NUOC CHAM
(VIETNAMESE DIPPING
SAUCE)

2 small Thai chilies, finely chopped
2 garlic cloves, chopped
3 tbsp rice vinegar
2 tbsp lime juice
2 tbsp fish sauce
1–2 tbsp sugar

Mix all of the ingredients and play with the amounts of sweet and sour
ingredients until you reach the desired flavor.

Let sit for 30 minutes before serving.

(A related sauce is nuoc mam, a Vietnamese fish sauce)

MAYONNAISE

2 egg yolks
½ tbsp Dijon mustard
1 tbsp white wine vinegar
¾–1 ⅓ cups (200–300 ml) rapeseed oil
salt and white pepper

Beat the yolks, mustard, and vinegar until the mixture becomes fluffy. Add the oil while stirring.
If the mayo becomes too thick, add a couple of drops of water.
Add vinegar, salt, and pepper to taste.

CHICKEN LIVER MOUSSE

¾ lb (400 g) chicken liver
¾ cup (200 g) butter
2 tbsp cognac
¼ cup (50 ml) cream
2 tbsp fish sauce
salt and pepper

Heat the pan with half of the butter and quickly fry the liver. Remove and put to the side. Save the butter in the pan.
When the liver has cooled, place it in a blender and add the rest of the butter along with the butter from the pan, the cognac, cream, and fish sauce.
Add salt and pepper to taste.
Place in a bowl and let sit in a cool place for 2 hours before serving.

PICKLED ROOT VEGETABLES

See the recipe for Knucklehead on page 47.

HOT DOG

THÜRINGER BRATWURST IN A BAGUETTE WITH SAUERKRAUT, PICKLED RED ONIONS, AND DEEP FRIED ONIONS

THÜRINGER BRATWURST IS A really good sausage to start with when mastering the art of sausage making. It's easy to switch out the seasonings as you wish. This sausage is prepared right before serving, so be sure to rinse the sausage immediately in cold water to avoid wrinkles. You can also prepare it uncooked and serve raw, but this will significantly diminish its shelf life. This recipe contains garlic sauerkraut, pickled red onions, and deep-fried onions. Extra everything is always best.

(Approx. 10–12 sausages)
2 lbs (1 kg) diced tenderloin
1 onion, finely chopped
3 garlic cloves, finely chopped
½ tbsp sugar
1 tbsp marjoram

½ tsp ground ginger
½ tsp nutmeg flower
½ tsp ground cilantro
1 tsp ground black pepper
1 tbsp non-iodized salt
½ cup (100 ml) whole milk, ice cold

Grind the meat on the coarsest setting.

Combine the meat, onions, spices, and milk and mix for about 10 minutes.

Grind the forcemeat again on the medium setting.

Fry a piece of the meat and sample.

Stuff the meat in pork casings and make sausages that are about 8 inches (20 cm) long.

Place the sausages in water that is 175°F (80°C) for 15 minutes. Make sure that the sausage reaches a temperature above 150°F (65°C) before you remove them.

Rinse the sausage in 60°F (15°C) water.

Let the sausage sit for 24 hours before serving so the flavors have ample time to develop. Store in the refrigerator, wrapped in paper.

Serve cooked, fried, or grilled depending on preference.

SERVING

Cook the sausages in sausage stock (see p.46) for 5–10 minutes. Place each bratwurst in a baguette and top with garlic sauerkraut, pickled red onions, and deep-fried onions. Finish it off with Dijon mustard.
(As previously mentioned, the sausages can be grilled, fried, or cooked.)

GARLIC SAUERKRAUT

2 tbsp butter
2 garlic cloves, chopped
1 lb (500 g) sauerkraut
2–3 tbsp vinegar
salt and pepper

Heat the butter in a pan and fry the chopped garlic. Add the cabbage and fry until it turns golden in color. Sample with vinegar, salt, and pepper. (You can serve it lukewarm or as a cold condiment.) You can also purchase sauerkraut at the store, but it is always tastier when it's homemade (see page 102)!

PICKLED RED ONIONS

4 red onions, wedged
½ cup (100 ml) vinegar
¾ cup (200 ml) sugar
¾ cup (200 ml) water

Heat all of the ingredients (except for the onions) in a saucepan. Stir constantly until the sugar has dissolved.
Remove from the stove and let cool.
Add the wedged onions and let them sit for 2–3 hours before serving.

DEEP-FRIED ONIONS

See the recipe for Chili All In on page 43.

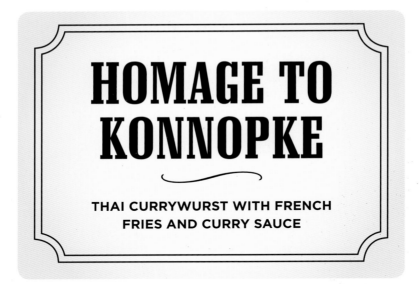

HOMAGE TO KONNOPKE

THAI CURRYWURST WITH FRENCH FRIES AND CURRY SAUCE

THE GERMANS KNOW THEIR sausage, and a couple of their greatest sausage concoctions are spotlighted in this book. This currywurst is a fantastic type of fast food. Street food *aus Berlin!*

The best currywurst is served in a small street kitchen in Prenzlauer Berg in East Berlin. Google it, go there, and go taste this delectable currywurst. Or make it yourself for some "Instant Berlin."

This sausage isn't an exact replica of the original, as this one contains flavors from Thailand and China as well as the traditional "Swedish" curry mix. It's an emulsion sausage, which means that after having ground the meat, you add cream—just like in the Wallenberger recipe.

A "regular" currywurst is boiled first before being fried. Let it simmer for 15–20 minutes before rinsing it in 50°F (15°C) water.

However, in this recipe, the currywurst will be fried.

(Approx. 40–50 sausages)
3 lbs (1 ½ kg) pork tenderloin, diced
½ cup (100 ml) cream
½ cup (100 ml) chopped cilantro leaves
1 tbsp non-iodized salt
1 tbsp mild green curry paste
1 tsp five spice powder
1 tsp curry powder
¼ tsp white pepper
⅔ cup (150 ml) ice-water

Grind the meat on the medium setting and place it in a mixer. Mix the meat, cream, and salt until it becomes a smooth batter. Add the spices, cilantro, and ice water and mix for another 5 minutes. Fry a piece of the forcemeat and sample.

Stuff the meat in sheep casings and make sausages that are 4 inches (10 cm) long.

Hang dry for 1–2 hours before refrigerating.

Let the sausages sit for 24 hours so the flavors have ample time to develop.

Fry the sausages before serving. Slice them if needed.

SERVING

We'll be making delicious homemade fries. These are the best French fries in the world! Relax. Just take your time and follow the recipe carefully. The trick is to start off by frying the potatoes at a low temperature before letting them dry. Then, you just fry them a second time—this time at a high temperature. The sausage gets fried and is served with orange seasoned curry sauce. You can also add homemade pretzels. *Sehr gut*!

FRENCH FRIES

4 large potatoes cut into sticks
deep-frying oil
salt

Place the potato sticks in cold water for approximately 30 minutes. Drain the water and rinse the potatoes.

Heat the oil in a deep fryer/pot to a temperature of 250°F (120°C). Add half of the potatoes and fry for 5 minutes.

Remove the fries and let them drain on paper towels. Repeat with the rest of the potato sticks. Place the fries on a tray and refrigerate overnight—this will extract the moisture. (Do not cover!)

Re-heat the fryer/pot with oil to a temperature of 340–355°F (170–180°C) and fry for 2–3 minutes until the fries turn golden.

Remove and drain on paper towels. Salt and serve.

PRETZELS

(10–12 pieces)
DOUGH
1 tsp dry yeast
1 tbsp brown sugar
2 ½–3 cups (600–700 ml) flour
1 tsp salt
1 cup (250 ml) milk, warmed to
    100°C (40°C)

TOPPING

1 egg
2 tsp milk
sea salt

Mix the dry ingredients in a bowl
and add the milk while stirring.
Knead the dough by hand for
10 minutes or in a stand mixer for
5 minutes. Let the dough rise in
a greased bowl covered in plastic
wrap for an hour.
Preheat the oven to 440°F (225°C).
Split the dough into 6 pieces and
roll into long sticks. Place under
a moist towel for 10 minutes and
let them rise before rolling them
out another half inch (1 cm). Form
pretzels into the desired shape.
If you have a steam oven, steam
them for 5 minutes. If you do not,
simply immerse them in boiling water for 10 minutes and let them dry.
Place the pretzels on a baking sheet
and brush with the beaten eggs and
milk. Sprinkle with salt.
Bake in the oven for 10–15 minutes
until they turn a nice brown color.

CURRY SAUCE

4 tbsp rapeseed oil
¾ cup (200 ml) tomato paste
4 tbsp curry powder
1 tbsp turmeric
1 tsp ground star anise
1 tsp cayenne pepper
¾ cup (200 ml) orange juice
¾ cup (200 ml) water
½ cube vegetable bouillon
2–3 tbsp honey
salt and pepper

Heat the tomato paste in the rapeseed oil. Add the curry, turmeric,
star anise, and cayenne pepper and
fry for another minute.
Add the orange juice,
water, and vegetable
bouillon. Let it boil
and then simmer
until it reaches the
consistency of
ketchup.
Add honey, salt,
and pepper to taste.
Serve either hot
or cold.

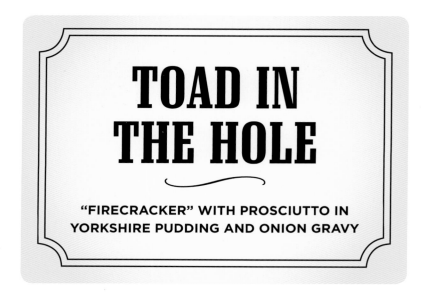

TOAD IN THE HOLE

"FIRECRACKER" WITH PROSCIUTTO IN YORKSHIRE PUDDING AND ONION GRAVY

IN ENGLAND, THESE PORK sausages are called "Bangers" because they crack during the preparation. This sausage is flavorful and filling and can be either fried or grilled. It's a classic mix of common flavors.

(Approx. 15–20 sausages)
2 lbs (1 kg) pork tenderloin
¾ lb (400 g) lard
⅔ lb (300 g) whole grain bread (soaked in water)
½ tsp ground nutmeg
1 tbsp ground nutmeg flower
1 tbsp ground ginger
1 tbsp crumbled sage
1 ½ tbsp non-iodized salt
2 tsp ground white pepper
⅔ cup (150 ml) ice-water

Grind the meat, lard, and whole wheat bread on the coarsest setting.

Mix the forcemeat with the spices and ice-water for about 10 minutes.

Fry a piece of the meat and sample.

Stuff the meat in pork casings and make sausages that are 3–4 inches (8–10 cm) long.

Hang dry for 1–2 hours before refrigerating.

Let the sausage sit for 24 hours before serving in order to allow ample time for the flavors to develop.

If you fry the sausage, it could crack (hence the name). However, in this recipe, the sausage will be baked in the oven inside of a Yorkshire pudding.

SERVING

You have to try this out! Make Yorkshire pudding batter and bake the sausages inside the pudding. The trick is to pour the batter into a really hot pan, since this will make the batter rise; the result will be very visually appealing. Roll the prosciutto around the sausages, fry them lightly, and then place them in the pudding and bake.

To reiterate: 1. Heat the pan. 2. Pour the batter. 3. Immerse the sausages in the batter.

For the ultimate experience, Toad in the Hole should be served with onion gravy.

YORKSHIRE PUDDING

4 eggs
1 ⅓ cups (300 ml) flour
1 ⅓ cups (300 ml) milk
salt
butter/oil

Beat the egg and milk and gradually add the flour. Make sure that the batter is smooth.

Add salt to taste.

Preheat the oven to 480°F (250°C) and heat the casserole dishes containing either butter or oil.

Remove from the oven, pour in the batter, and top each pudding with a sausage. Return to the oven and bake for 20 minutes.

Remove and serve.

P.S. It's important to heat the butter/oil in the dishes before adding the batter.

ONION GRAVY

2 red onions, peeled and thinly sliced
2 garlic cloves, peeled and thinly sliced
2 tbsp butter
1 tbsp unrefined sugar
½ cup (100 ml) balsamic vinegar
1 tbsp beef stock
¾ cup (200 ml) water
salt and black pepper

Heat butter in a saucepan and sweat the onion and garlic. When the onion becomes transparent, add the sugar and let it sweat for another minute.
Add vinegar and let half of it evaporate.
Add the meat stock and water, bring to a boil, then add salt and pepper to taste.

OVER-THE-TOP BACON

BACON AND PAPRIKA SAUSAGE IN BACON
BREAD WITH MUSTARD SLAW, BACON
CRUMBLES, AND CHILI KETCHUP

WE ARE COMPLETELY IN love with bacon! It's one of those things you can easily fry at any point of the day. (Try doing that with herring. . . .) For the ultimate bacon flavor, add fried bacon to the sausage meat. You may also want to add the drippings!

The fennel and the paprika complement each other very well. This sausage is rather spicy, but you can regulate that to taste by modifying the amount of cayenne pepper and chili flakes you use—but we don't think you'll want to!

You can easily accomplish that curved formation by attaching the ends of the sausage with a toothpick until ready to fry or grill.

(Approx. 15–20 sausages)
2 lbs (1 kg) pork tenderloin, diced
²⁄₃ lb (300 g) crispy, lightly smoked bacon, shredded
1 cup (250 ml) chopped parsley
1 tbsp crushed fennel seeds
1 tbsp cayenne pepper
2 tsp chili flakes
3 tbsp Hungarian paprika
2 tbsp Pimentón de La Vera, Picante
1 tsp non-iodized salt
1 tbsp coarsely ground black pepper
1 cup (250 ml) red wine, ice-cold

Grind the meat on the finest setting.

Mix the meat with the bacon, spices, and red wine for 10 minutes.

Fry a piece of the forcemeat and sample.

Stuff the meat in sheep casings and make sausages that are 8 inches (20 cm) long. Twist them and fasten with a toothpick.

Dry on an oven rack for 1–2 hours before refrigerating.

Let the sausages sit for 24 hours in order to allow ample time for the flavors to develop.

Fry or grill before serving.

SERVING

Fry or grill the sausages and serve in homemade buns. Add coleslaw and top with bacon crumbles and chili ketchup.

BACON HAMBURGER BUN

1 cup (250 ml) milk
½ cup (100 ml) water
3 ½ tbsp (50 g) butter
3–3 ½ cups (700–800 ml) flour
1 package (½ oz [12 g]) active dry yeast
5 tsp (25 ml) sugar
1 tsp salt
2 eggs
5 oz (140 g) crispy, lightly smoked bacon, shredded

Heat the milk, water, and butter in a saucepan until it reaches a temperature of 120°F (50°C).

Meanwhile, mix 1 ⅔ cups of the flour with the yeast, sugar, and salt in a bowl.

Add the milk mixture along with half of the fried bacon and knead the dough for a couple of minutes.

Add an egg, mix thoroughly, and gradually stir in the flour.

Run the dough in a mixer for 8–10 minutes until it becomes elastic.

Split the dough into 12–16 pieces and make buns. Place on a baking sheet and let them rise under a towel for about 20–30 minutes.

Beat the other egg and brush onto the buns. Sprinkle the rest of the bacon on top. Bake at 390°F (200°C) for 10–12 minutes.

Let the buns cool before serving.

MUSTARD SLAW

1 Bok Choi, shredded
½ cup (100 ml) mayonnaise
½ cup (100 ml) yellow mustard
½ cup (100 ml) apple cider vinegar
½ cup (100 ml) sugar
1–2 tbsp salt
2 tsp freshly ground black pepper
2 tsp brown mustard seeds

Place the shredded cabbage in water and
add a pinch of salt. Let sit for 30 minutes.
Drain out the water with a colander and
squeeze out the rest of the liquid.
Mix with the rest of the ingredients and
sample. Toss the slaw and place in the refrigerator for 30 minutes before serving.

BACON CRISP

1 package of bacon, shredded
freshly ground black pepper

Place the bacon strips in a pan and fry at
medium temperature until they become
crispy. Add black pepper and let them dry
on paper towels.

CHILI KETCHUP

See the recipe for Blood Sausage in Madrid
on page 59.

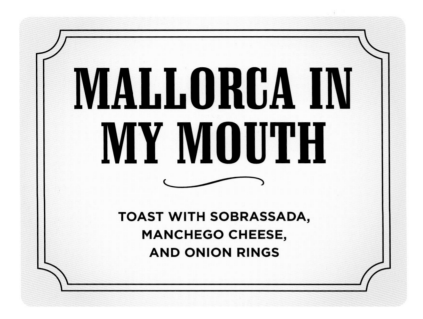

MALLORCA IN MY MOUTH

TOAST WITH SOBRASSADA, MANCHEGO CHEESE, AND ONION RINGS

THIS RECIPE HAILS FROM another of Johan's travels: "I discovered this sausage for the first time at a breakfast place in Barcelona. I couldn't get enough of it, and I still buy a ton whenever I'm in the neighborhood." Sobrassada comes from Mallorca and is a soft sausage that makes a great spread. As with Botifarra, Sobrassada's distinct flavor is courtesy of the Spanish paprika. The added cayenne pepper gives it some extra heat.

(Approx. 4–5 sausages)
1 ½ lbs (750 g) pork (e.g. pork shoulder), diced
½ lb (300 g) salted pork, diced
⅓ lb (150 g) beef (e.g. chuck roll)
6 tbsp Pimentón de La Vera, Dulce (sweet paprika)
1 tbsp cayenne pepper (optional)
2 ½ tbsp non-iodized salt
1 tbsp coarsely ground black pepper

Grind the pork on the coarsest setting and the beef on the finest setting. Mix the two meats with the spices for about 10–15 minutes.
Stuff the forcemeat in sheep casings and make sausages that are 15 inches (40 cm) long. Tie each end of the sausage.

Tie a string around the sausage about 2–4 inches (5–10 cm) down. Fold down the shorter end (for a reference picture, see page 18). Let the sausages hang dry in a cool location (about 60°F [15°C]) for 1–2 weeks until they feel solid.

Store in the refrigerator and serve as a spread or enjoy as is.

SERVING

The best way to consume this sausage is on toast. Spread a generous amount of sobrassada on a piece of toast and top with manchego cheese and a second piece of toast. Place in a panini press until the cheese melts and a sausage begins to seep out from the sides. Serve with onion rings. "Haaallelujah and good morning!!"

ONION RINGS

3–4 large onions, peeled
2 cups (500 ml) flour
⅔ cup (150 ml) cornmeal
½ cup (100 ml) corn starch
2 ½ tbsp baking powder
1 tbsp dried parsley
1 tbsp salt
deep-frying oil
⅔ cup (150 ml) milk
⅔ cup (150 ml) heavy cream

Slice the onions ¾ to 1 inch (2–3 cm) thick and soak in a bowl of water for at least 30 minutes.

Mix a cup and a half of the flour with the cornmeal, cornstarch, baking powder, parsley, and salt.

Heat the oil to 340–355°F (170–180°C). Remove the onion rings from the water.

Mix the milk and cream in a bowl and place the rest of the flour in a separate bowl.

Drop 4–5 of the onion rings in the flour, dip them in the milk/cream mixture, and finally, in the flour mixture.

Deep fry the onion rings for 2–3 minutes or until they turn golden.

Remove and drain on paper towels before serving.

Nötchorizo 125 gram 2:

Nötjättegrill 125 gram 2:

Lammkorv 90 gram 2:

Kycklingkorv 50 gram 1

BEEF

FIRE HOSE

JESPER'S HOT DOG WITH COUSCOUS AND MINT YOGURT

AS THE NAME INDICATES, this sausage is hot! The flavor stems from five types of chili and hot paprika. Make sure the chili is well mixed with the meat so the flavors have a chance to develop gradually rather than in the first bite.

The name "Jesper's Hot Dog" comes from our co-author—he's absolutely crazy about chili. (Hot is the way to go!) For both Jesper and other spice lovers: This one is for you!

This sausage is reminiscent of merguez sausage, but it's made from beef and is slightly smokier.

(Approx. 14–16 sausages)
1 onion, chopped
2 garlic cloves, chopped
1 stalk of celery, chopped
2 tbsp olive oil
2 tbsp sambal oelek
1 tsp ground ancho chili
2 Thai chilies, sliced
1 tsp chili flakes
1 tsp Tabasco
1 tbsp hot Hungarian paprika
1 ½ lbs (750 g) beef (e.g. chuck roll)
½ lb (250 g) lard
2 tbsp honey
2 tbsp liquid smoke
1 ½ tsp non-iodized salt
½ tsp freshly ground black pepper
⅔ cup (150 ml) pilsner or pale lager, ice-cold

Heat oil in a pan and sweat the onion, garlic, and celery until they become transparent.

Add the chili spices and paprika and fry for a couple of minutes. Turn off the heat and let cool.

Grind the meat and spice mixture on the finest setting. Mix the forcemeat with the rest of the spices, then fry a piece and sample. Spicy enough for you?

Stuff the meat in sheep casings and make sausages that are 6 inches (15 cm) long.

Hang dry for about 2 hours before refrigerating.

Fry or grill before serving.

SERVING

You should grill this sausage. It's quick to do and makes it even tastier. We will be serving it with Middle Eastern couscous, roasted vegetables, and mint yogurt. This is the perfect spring or summer dish!

COUSCOUS WITH ROASTED VEGETABLES

1 lb (500 g) vegetables (e.g. bell pepper, squash, onion, garlic, etc.)
4 servings of couscous
1 lemon
½ cup (100 ml) finely chopped parsley
1 tbsp chopped mint
salt and pepper

Place the cut vegetables on a baking sheet and drizzle with olive oil. Roast in the oven for about 20 minutes at a temperature of 400°F (200°C).
Prepare the couscous according to the instructions.
Stir the roasted vegetables into the freshly made couscous.
Add olive oil, lemon juice, salt, and pepper to taste. Garnish with some mint and parsley.
Let sit for 30 minutes before serving.

MINT YOGURT

¾ cup (200 ml) Turkish yogurt
½ red chili, shredded
½ cup (100 ml) finely shredded mint
Zest of 1 lime
Salt and pepper

Mix all ingredients and sample with salt and pepper. Let sit for 30 minutes before serving.

WALLENBERGER

WALLENBERGER WITH PEA PURÉE, LINGONBERRY KETCHUP, AND PICKLES

IF YOU ARE A fan of the Swedish movie *Jönssonligan*, this is the sausage for you. It's actually a Wallenberger—a beloved Swedish dish—stuffed in a casing.

Make sure that the forcemeat stays cold throughout the preparation. You can choose to either fry it immediately or let it simmer and cool before refrying in butter.

(Approx. 8–10 sausages)
1 ½ lbs (800 g) veal, diced
1 ½ tsp non-iodized salt
1 tsp five-spice powder
½ tsp freshly ground white pepper
8 egg yolks
2 ½ cups (600 ml) heavy cream

Grind the veal two times on the finest setting. After grinding, the force-meat should be mixed in a blender with salt, spices, and egg yolks. When the forcemeat gets tough, add the cream. Mix until it becomes a batter. Fry a piece of the meat and sample.

Stuff the meat in pork casings and make sausages that are 6–8 inches (15–20 cm) long.

Poach the sausages until their centers reach a temperature of 150°F (65°C). Remove from the water and immediately rinse in cold water. Store in the refrigerator and fry before serving.

SERVING

This recipe mimics the flavors of the classic Wallenberger dish. However, this recipe uses pea purée rather than mashed potatoes, in addition to smoky lingonberry ketchup and pickles. For a luxurious garnish, add some browned butter. This is gourmet food!

GARLIC PEA PURÉE

2 cups (500 ml) frozen peas, thawed
1 garlic clove
1 tsp salt
½ tsp black pepper
½ cup (100 ml) olive oil
½ cup (100 ml) grated parmesan
salt and pepper

Mix the peas, garlic, and spices in a blender before adding the olive oil and parmesan. Add more salt and pepper if you feel it needs it. Heat the purée before serving.

LINGONBERRY KETCHUP

7 oz (200 g) lingonberries.
1 scallion, finely chopped
½ of a chipotle chili, sliced
½ cup (100 ml) sugar
¼ cup (50 ml) red wine vinegar
¾ cup (200 ml) Coca-Cola
salt and white pepper

Place all of the ingredients in a saucepan.
Bring to a boil and let simmer for 1 hour.
Sample with salt and pepper and balance
the taste with sugar and vinegar.

PICKLED CUCUMBER WITH CHILI

½ cup (100 ml) vinegar
1 cup (250 ml) water
¾ cup (200 ml) sugar
1 cucumber, thinly sliced
1 green chili, thinly sliced
½ cup (100 ml) finely chopped parsley

Combine the vinegar, sugar, and water. Make
sure the sugar dissolves.
Add the cucumber, chili, and parsley. Let sit
for 30 minutes before serving.

THE AVERAGE JOE

RED WINE SAUSAGE WITH FRENCH FRIES AND BÉARNAISE

THE PLAN WAS TO make a delicious sausage to go with the Swedes' favorite condiments: French fries and béarnaise. Said and done—here it is! In order to make the forcemeat a little juicier, add some fat from beef or lard. Let the meat marinate overnight before grinding. It should have a rather loose consistency, but be sure to strain out the wine before grinding. Ideally, the meat should be stuffed in sheep casings in order to make long and thin sausages. If you want, you can also make thicker sausages with pork casings.

(The number of sausages depends on the type of casing)

1 ¾ (800 g) beef (e.g. chuck roll)

½ lb (200 g) beef fat

1 red onion, sliced

2 garlic cloves

1 tbsp tarragon

2 tbsp red wine vinegar

1 ¼ cups (300 ml) red wine

1 tsp cayenne pepper

½ cup (100 ml) chopped parsley

½ cup (100 ml) breadcrumbs

2 tsp non-iodized salt

black pepper

Place everything except the parsley, breadcrumbs, salt, and pepper in a bowl and let sit overnight. Strain and save the liquid. Grind on the coarsest setting. Mix the forcemeat with half of the liquid and the parsley, breadcrumbs, salt, and pepper.

Fry a piece of the meat and sample.

Stuff the meat in sheep or pork casings and make them as long as you wish.

Let dry for 2 hours before refrigerating.

Fry or grill before serving.

SERVING

This dish has all the traditional Swedish flavors: Steak, French fries, and béarnaise! But instead of steak, we're substituting sausages marinated in red wine. What can go wrong? Absolutely nothing!

Of course, this delicious sausage should be served with homemade fries and béarnaise. We're talking world class!

As for beverage choice—red wine, obviously. (You ought to have a little less than a cup left in the bottle, so drink up!)

FRENCH FRIES

See the recipe on page 70.

BÉARNAISE SAUCE

1 shallot, finely chopped
1 tbsp tarragon
½ tsp crushed white pepper
2 tbsp red wine vinegar
¼ cup (50 ml) water
3 egg yolks
1 cup (250 g) melted, lukewarm butter
1 tbsp chopped parsley
salt and pepper

Place the shallot, tarragon, white pepper, vinegar, and water in a saucepan. Let simmer until the shallot has absorbed the liquid.

Let the shallot cool, then add the egg yolks and whisk until the mixture becomes light and fluffy. Add the melted butter carefully while stirring. Add the parsley and some extra tarragon. Add salt and pepper to taste.

Make sure the sauce stays lukewarm and stir occasionally until ready to serve.

UTOPENEC

PICKLED MARJORAM SAUSAGE ON A BAGUETTE

THE NAME REFERS TO the dish itself and not the sausage. The recipe was originally Czech and should be made with Thüringer Bratwurst—a pork sausage consisting of veal, pork, and some added herbs and beer.

(Approx. 10–12 sausages)
2 tsp butter
1 onion, finely chopped
1 tsp dried marjoram
2 tsp dried parsley
½ lb (750 g) veal, diced
½ lb (250 g) pork tenderloin, cubed
1 ½ tsp non-iodized salt
½ cup (100 ml) pilsner or pale lager, ice-cold

Heat the butter in a pan and sweat the onions until they become transparent.

Remove from the stove, add the marjoram and parsley, and let the mixture cool.

Grind the veal and the onion twice on the finest setting. Mix the forcemeat with the pieces of veal and add salt and pepper to taste.

Fry a piece of the meat and sample.

Stuff the forcemeat in pork casings and make sausages that are 4 inches (10 cm) long.

Poach the sausage in "preserving juice" until the middle sections reach a temperature of 150°F (65°C). Remove from the stove and let cool.

PRESERVING JUICE

1 tbsp mustard seeds
4 bay leaves
8 black peppercorns
1 stalk of celery, sliced
1 onion, thinly sliced
2 cups (500 ml) white wine vinegar
1 cup (250 ml) water
salt

Mix all ingredients in a saucepan. Bring to a boil and let simmer for 5 minutes.

Bring to a boil again, then remove the pan from the heat and add the sausage.

Replace on the flame and bring the solution to a boil once more. Remove from the heat and let cool with the lid on.

Refrigerate for two days before serving.

After two days, strain the solution and add some fresh vegetables and herbs for a great garnish.

SERVING

This dish should be served according to the Czech tradition. Therefore, it's important that the sausage be allowed enough time to sit in the white wine vinegar. Use a fork to remove the sausages from the solution. (Do not dip your fingers in the mixture! The bacteria on your skin can react with the solution and will reduce shelf life.) Garnish with some green herbs or vegetables and serve on a baguette. The sour taste will leave you craving a big glass of beer (also in perfect accordance with the Czech tradition!).

WURST FEST

BRING IT ON WITH GERMAN POTATO SALAD, SAUERKRAUT, PICKLES, HORSERADISH, AND MUSTARD

THIS SAUSAGE IS A take on the traditional beef brisket and has almost all the same flavors.

It tastes delicious and it keeps a terrific red color throughout the preparation process.

Make sure to wash the vegetables before grinding, as this will give the sausage the perfect flavor and consistency.

(Approx. 35–40 sausages)
2 lbs (1 kg) brined beef brisket, diced
1 onion, sliced
2 garlic cloves
1 carrot, grated
2 stalks of celery, sliced
2 bay leaves
½ tbsp non-iodized salt
1 tsp crushed white pepper

Grind the brisket, onion, garlic, carrot, celery, and bay leaves on the medium setting.

Mix the forcemeat with salt and white pepper (go light on the salt—the brisket is already quite salty).

Fry a piece of the meat and sample.

Stuff the meat in sheep casings and make sausages that are 4 inches (10cm) long.

Let dry for 2 hours before refrigerating.

Poach for 10 minutes in sausage stock (see page 46 for instructions) before serving. They should reach a temperature of 140°F (60°C).

SERVING

This sausage is small enough that you can eat many of them in one go. Poaching cooks the vegetables inside the sausage, making them very juicy. It is possible to "pre-poach" the sausages before refrigerating and poach them again right before serving. The dish should be served with a lukewarm German potato salad, sauerkraut, pickles, some freshly grated horseradish, and mustard! *Alles Gut*!

SAUERKRAUT

4 ½ lbs (2 kg) shredded cabbage
2 ½ tbsp coarse, non-iodized salt
3 tbsp processed sour milk

First of all, DON'T use aluminum bowls and make sure to keep everything really clean throughout the cooking process.

Place the cabbage in a stainless steel bowl.

Add the salt and mix with a wooden spoon or rubber gloves. Mix until the salt has dissolved and a liquid appears. When this happens, pour in the sour milk.

Place the mixture on a plate and weigh it down so that the cabbage is pressed into the liquid.

Let sit at room temperature (68–72°F [20–22°C]) for 1–3 weeks. Make sure that the cabbage is always immersed in the liquid.

When the cabbage is ready, chill it in a cool location and again make sure that the cabbage is immersed in the liquid.

When serving, rinse quickly if it is too sour.

GERMAN POTATO SALAD

8 ½ cups (2 liters) chicken broth
2 lbs (1 kg) sliced potatoes
3 tbsp white wine vinegar
¼ cup (50 ml) olive oil
2 tbsp Dijon mustard
⅓ cup chopped parsley
3 scallions, sliced
3 tbsp capers
1 garlic clove, finely chopped
salt and white pepper

Bring the broth to a boil and let the potatoes simmer until they are almost done (al dente).

Drain out the broth but save a fourth of a cup of it. Mix this with the vinegar, oil, and mustard.

Add the lukewarm potatoes and the parsley, scallions, capers, and garlic. Add salt and pepper to taste.

PICKLES WITH CHILI

4 ¼ cups (1 liter) water
⅓ cup (75 ml) sea salt
2 lbs (1 kg) rinsed cucumber
1 bundle of dill, chopped into
    small pieces
2–4 Thai chilies, sliced
2 garlic cloves, crushed

Mix the water and the salt in a bowl big enough to accommodate at least double the amount of liquid. Stir until the salt has dissolved. Place the cucumbers in the salted water, then add the dill, chilies, and garlic. Make sure that the cucumbers are immersed in the water. Cover with a lid or aluminum foil and refrigerate. It can be served after 24 hours, but the longer it's allowed to sit, the better it will taste.

OH DEER!

DEER HUNTER IN A BUN
WITH PICKLED MUSHROOMS AND
HOT HONEY MUSTARD

THIS IS A DELICIOUS sausage made from reindeer meat. Since reindeer meat is rather lean, this sausage also contains some added pork for extra juice. It should be served with traditional Swedish flavors, such as juniper berry, clove, parsley, and black pepper.

(Approx. 8–10 sausages)
1 lb (500 g) reindeer meat, diced (alternately, try venison or any other type of game)
1 lb (500 g) pork tenderloin, diced
¾ cup (200 ml) chopped parsley
6 crushed juniper berries
½ tsp ground nutmeg
½ tsp ground clove
1 tsp garlic powder
1 tbsp non-iodized salt
1 tsp freshly ground black pepper
¾ cup (200 ml) ice-water

Grind the meat on the coarsest setting.
Mix the ground meat with the spices and the water for about 10 minutes.
Fry a piece of the meat and sample.
Stuff the forcemeat in pork casings and make sausages that are 6 inches (15 cm) long.
Hang dry for 1–2 hours before refrigerating.
Ideally, you should let the sausages sit for 24 hours before serving to allow ample time for the flavors to develop.
Fry or grill when it's time to eat!

SERVING

This dish calls for some traditional flavors straight from the woods. So, serve it on a bun with pickled mushrooms and hot honey mustard. Downright delicious.

PICKLED MUSHROOMS

½ lb (1 liter) mixed mushrooms, rinsed
2 tsp salt
2 cinnamon sticks (2 inches [5 cm] each)
3 slices of fresh ginger
10 black peppercorns
1 ¼ cups (300 ml) mushroom drippings (from the mushrooms)
⅔ cup (150 ml) white vinegar
⅔ cup (150 ml) sugar

Salt the mushrooms and place in a saucepan. Let them simmer with a lid for 10 minutes. Pour out the drippings and save one and a fourth (300 ml) cups. Let the mushrooms drain completely.

Place the mushrooms in jars with the cinnamon sticks, cloves, ginger, and black peppercorns.

Bring the mushroom drippings to a boil along with the vinegar and sugar. Pour the hot stock over the mushrooms, put a lid on them, and let sit until the next day.

Strain the contents of the jars and bring the stock to a boil again.

Return the mushrooms to the cleaned glass jars and add the stock.

Put the lids back on the jars and refrigerate.

HOT DOG BUNS

1 cup (250 ml) milk
½ cup (100 ml) water
¼ cup (50 g) butter
3–3 ½ cups (700–800 ml) flour
1 packet (12 g) dry yeast
1 ½ tbsp (25 ml) granulated sugar
1 tsp salt
1 + 1 eggs

In a saucepan, heat the milk, water, and butter to 125°F (50°C) in a saucepan.

Meanwhile, in a stand mixer, mix one and two thirds of a cup of the flour and the yeast, sugar, and salt. Pour in the milk while stirring. Add one of the eggs and mix thoroughly. Then add the rest of the flour, half a cup at a time.

Work the dough in the stand mixer for 8–10 minutes until it becomes elastic. Split the dough into 12–16 pieces and form into hot dog buns. Place on a baking sheet and let rise under a cloth for 20–30 minutes.

Whisk the remaining egg and brush the buns.

Bake them in the oven at of 400°F (200°C) for 10–12 minutes.

Remove from the oven and let them cool down.

HOT HONEY MUSTARD

See the recipe for Knucklehead on page 47.

MOOSE ON THE LOOSE

FRIED MOOSE MEAT IN A BAGUETTE
WITH LINGONBERRY KETCHUP, PICKLES,
AND DEEP-FRIED ONIONS.

SWEDEN IS LUCKY TO have plenty of moose in its forests, but unfortunately they're often hunted and killed for meat. With this delicious sausage melting in your mouth, you'll feel that the moose won't have died in vain.

Inspired by the fall hunting season and some foreign influences, Johan composed this recipe with apples and ajvar relish.

In order to increase the juiciness, the meat is mixed with some salted pork (ideally the piece with the highest fat content). If you want some extra heat, add chili flakes.

(Approx. 25–30 sausages)
2 lbs (1 kg) moose meat, diced
½ lb (200 g) salted pork, diced
1 apple, peeled and cored
2 tsp non-iodized salt
¾ cup (200 ml) heavy cream
½ cup (100 ml) ajvar relish (mild or hot)
1 tsp chili flakes (optional)
2 tsp coarsely ground black peppercorns

Grind both meats and the apple on the medium setting and place in a blender.

Blend with the salt and heavy cream for 5 minutes.

Add the ajvar relish, chili flakes (optional), and black pepper.

Fry a piece of the meat and sample.

Stuff the meat in pork casings and make sausages that are 1–2 inches (3–5 cm) long. Tie with twine.

Hang dry for 1–2 hours before refrigerating.

Ideally, you should let the sausages sit for 24 hours before serving to allow ample time for the flavors to develop.

Fry, grill, or boil before serving.

SERVING

This moose sausage is supposed to be served as a snack with beer. Fry and serve in a baguette with lingonberry ketchup, pickles, and deep-fried onions.

LINGONBERRY KETCHUP
PICKLED CUCUMBER WITH CHILI

See the recipe for Wallenberger on page 93.

DEEP-FRIED ONIONS

See the recipe for Chili All In on page 43.

SKOGAHOLM

**VENISON SALAMI ON
BREAD WITH SAUERKRAUT, PICKLED
RED ONIONS, AND HORSERADISH**

IT'S TIME TO ONCE again mix the lean game meat with pork—but this time with pure pork fat. If you have access to deer fat, use that instead. We'll show you our tricks to make "salami" ready to be enjoyed at any time.

Since not everyone is able to properly smoke the sausage at home, we'll cheat and use liquid smoke instead and then dry them in the oven.

Read more about access to artificial casings under "Nice 2 Know" on page 184.

(Approx. 3–4 large sausages)
2 lbs (1 kg) venison, diced
½ lb (250 g) lard, diced
1 onion, grated
2 tbsp dried tarragon
2 tbsp raw sugar
1 tbsp liquid smoke
2 tsp non-iodized salt
2 tsp black peppercorns
¾ cup (200 ml) ice-water

Grind the meat, lard, and onion on the coarsest setting.

Mix the forcemeat with the spices, liquid smoke, and ice water for about 15 minutes.

Fry a piece of the meat and sample.

Stuff the meat in artificial casings and tie with twine.

Hang dry the salami in the oven at a temperature of 160°F (70°C) for 4–5 hours. Quickly rinse the sausages in cold water until they reach a temperature of 60°F (15°C).

Let sit for 24 hours before serving to allow ample time for the flavors to develop.

Slice before placing on atop a piece of bread.

SERVING

A delicious sandwich can never be wrong. This recipe calls for a very Swedish loaf of syrup bread, topped with pickled red onions and freshly grated horseradish. Is there a better way to enjoy the wild while waiting for seconds?

SAUERKRAUT

See the recipe for Wurst Fest on page 102.

PICKLED RED ONIONS

See the recipe for Hot Dog on page 66.

NILSSON

LAMB SAUSAGE ON FRIED BREAD WITH CARAMELIZED ONIONS AND A FRIED EGG

THIS LAMB SAUSAGE RESEMBLES the classic merguez sausage with some of the same North African flavors. It contains beef, but that can be switched out.

Harissa derives from Tunisia and is a very hot chili paste. Be careful or the heat of the chili may cause problems! The recipe also contains the flavors of cumin, marjoram, and fennel. It's best served grilled.

The sandwich is named after this book's photographer Pepe Nilsson, who particularly enjoys this sandwich.

(Approx. 10–12 sausages)
2 lbs (1 kg) lamb meat, diced
½ lb (250 g) chuck roll, diced
½ cup (100 ml) sliced onions
3 garlic cloves
½ tbsp harissa paste
1 tbsp paprika, hot

1 tsp dried oregano
1 tsp ground fennel seeds
1 tsp dried marjoram
½ tsp ground cumin
2 ½ tsp salt
1 tsp freshly ground black pepper
⅔ cup (150 ml) ice-water

Grind the meat, onion, and garlic on the coarsest setting. Mix forcemeat, spices, and water for 10 minutes.

Fry a piece of the meat and sample.

Stuff the meat in sheep casings and make sausages that are 6 inches (15 cm) long.

Hang dry for 1–2 hours before refrigerating.

Ideally, you should let the sausages sit for 24 hours before serving so the flavors can develop fully.

Grill and serve immediately.

SERVING

Grill the sausages. Fry a piece of bread in butter and make a simple tomato salad to place on top. Add the caramelized onions and then the sausages. Place a fried egg on top and suddenly you have a gut-busting sandwich for dinner!

TOMATO SALAD

3 tomatoes, finely sliced
1 bunch of chives, chopped
1–2 tbsp olive oil
1 tbsp red wine vinegar
salt and pepper

Layer the sliced tomatoes on a plate and sprinkle the chopped chives on top. Add olive oil and vinegar and season with salt and pepper to taste.

CARAMELIZED ONIONS

2 yellow onions, thinly sliced
2 red onions, thinly sliced
1 garlic clove, finely sliced
¼ cup (50 g) butter
2 tbsp sugar
a splash of beer
salt and white pepper

Heat the butter in a pan and fry the onions on a medium flame until they soften (or for about 10 minutes).
Add the sugar and let it dissolve into the onions. Add a splash of beer and let it be absorbed into the onions.
Add salt and pepper to taste.
Serve warm, cold, or lukewarm.

GREEK PLATE DOWN UNDER

THE AUSSIE WITH OVEN-ROASTED POTATOES, TZATZIKI AND DIJONNAISE

JOHAN WAS TAUGHT THIS recipe when he was studying abroad in Adelaide, Australia. Oddly enough, it contains distinctly Greek flavors. And the recipe works just as well for making hamburgers.

Make sure that the feta cheese is crushed when mixing with the basil so that the sausage contains chunks of feta.

(Approx. 18–20 sausages)
2 lbs (1 kg) lamb meat, diced
¼ lb (200 g) lard, diced
½ cup (100 ml) finely chopped sundried tomatoes
¾ cup (200 ml) feta cheese, crumbled
3 tbsp basil leaves, finely chopped
1 tbsp rosemary, finely chopped
3 garlic cloves, chopped
1 tbsp non-iodized salt
½ tsp coarsely ground black pepper
⅔ cup (150 ml) ice-water

Grind the meat and the lard on the coarsest setting.

Mix the forcemeat with the tomatoes, feta cheese, spices, and water for about 5 minutes.

Fry a piece of the meat and sample.

Stuff the meat in pork casings and make sausages that are 4 inches (10 cm) long.

Hang dry for 1–2 hours before refrigerating.

Let the sausages sit for 24 hours before serving in order to allow the flavors ample time to develop.

Grill or fry and serve immediately.

SERVING

This is easy to prepare. Roast the potatoes in the oven and serve the sausage grilled or fried alongside tzatziki and some dijonnaise. Dig in and taste some Greek food from down under!

OVEN-ROASTED POTATOES

2 lbs (1 kg) potatoes, thinly sliced
½ cup (100 ml) olive oil
salt and pepper

Heat a deep baking sheet in the oven at 440°F (225°C).

Rinse the potato slices in cold water. Dry and mix in a bowl with olive oil, salt, and pepper.

Remove the baking sheet, distribute the potatoes evenly, and quickly return to the oven.

Bake for 15–20 minutes while stirring occasionally. The potatoes are ready once they have turned golden in color.

TZATZIKI

2 cucumbers, shredded and dried
2 cups (500 g) Turkish yogurt
3 tbsp olive oil
1 tbsp chopped parsley
1 tbsp chopped mint
1 tbsp chopped dill
2–3 garlic cloves
2–3 tbsp lemon juice
salt and pepper

Mix the shredded cucumbers with some salt and
let drain in a colander for an hour.
Squeeze out the rest of the liquid from the cucumbers and place in a bowl.
Stir in the rest of the ingredients. Add salt and pepper to taste.

DIJONNAISE

2 egg yolks
½ tbsp Dijon mustard
1 tbsp white wine vinegar
¾–1 ¼ cups (200–300 ml) rapeseed
    oil salt
white pepper
¼–½ cup (50–100 ml) Dijon mustard

Start by making the mayonnaise:
Beat the egg yolks, mustard, and vinegar.
Gradually add the oil while stirring.
If the mayonnaise becomes too thick, add a couple of drops of water.
Add salt and pepper to taste.
Finally, mix the Dijon mustard into the mayonnaise.

(POLSK JAKTWURST)
NÖTBRATWURST ....
OVES PEPPARKORV ....
ÄKTA SALSICCIA 35
ORT OCH VILT 35

UNNBRÖDSRULLAR
KOKT/GRILLAD
TJOCK KORV 60

KOKT/GRILLAD 40   ENKEL
TJOCK KORV 50   DUBBEL

TILLBEHÖR
BOSTONGURKA 5
SURKMAJONNÄS 5
SAKSALLAD 10
SORKRL 5
MOS 10

DRYCKER
• SMAKIS ....
• BURK 33 cl. ....
• PET 50 cl. ....
• PUCKO 20 cl. ....

POULTRY

DUCK DUCK

**PEPPERY DUCK AND CRANBERRY
SAUSAGE WITH CORN ON THE COB,
MANGO KETCHUP, AND GARLIC BREAD**

DUCK IS DELICIOUS AND should be used in more recipes and in more
types of food than are traditional. It makes for a fantastic sausage because
duck meat contains a lot of natural fat, adding plenty of flavor and succu-
lence.

Johan: "This is F----- delicious! So flavorful! Great balance between sweet
and sour!"

(Approx. 18–20 sausages)
2 lbs (1 kg) duck breast (with the fat), diced
1 onion, grated
½ cup (100 ml) parsley, chopped
½ cup (100 ml) dried cranberries, coarsely chopped
½ tsp crushed white pepper
½ tsp crushed black pepper
2 tsp crushed green peppercorns (in brine)
2 tsp brown mustard seeds
1 tsp dried sage
2 tsp non-iodized salt
½ cup (100 ml) cranberry juice, ice-cold

Grind the duck breast on the medium setting. Mix forcemeat with onion, parsley, cranberry, spices, and cranberry juice for about 10 minutes.
Fry a piece of the meat and sample.
Stuff the meat in sheep casings and make sausages that are 8–10 inches (20–25 cm) long.
Hang dry for 1–2 hours and then store in the refrigerator overnight. This will allow ample time for the flavors to develop.
Fry, grill, or boil before serving.

SERVING

This is a no-brainer. Serve grilled with sweet condiments like freshly grilled corn on the cob, mango ketchup, and some garlic bread. Simple, easy, and delicious!

MANGO KETCHUP

¾ cup (200 ml) mango chutney
½–1 tbsp apple cider vinegar

Mix until smooth. Add vinegar to taste.

GARLIC BREAD

4–6 slices of bread
3 garlic cloves, finely chopped
½ cup (100 ml) olive oil
¼ cup (50 g) butter
salt and pepper

Heat the garlic, oil, and butter in a saucepan until the garlic turns light brown. Remove from the stove and add salt and pepper to taste.
Brush the mixture onto the bread and grill on both sides.

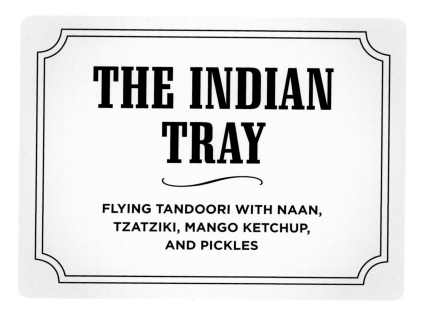

THE INDIAN TRAY

FLYING TANDOORI WITH NAAN, TZATZIKI, MANGO KETCHUP, AND PICKLES

DOES A SAUSAGE HAVE to come stuffed in a casing, skin, or wrap in order to be called a sausage? No, no!! As long as it's oblong and has two ends, it is—in our opinion—a sausage! Anyway, here is a culinary celebration of India. We don't care if it's called a sausage or otherwise—this meal is a total blast!

In this recipe, the meat is formed into a sausage shape and is placed on skewers. It's important that the "sausages" sit in the refrigerator for a couple of hours before being grilled or fried.

The Indian flavors work well with the turkey and chicken.

Don't forget to include the skin in the grinding process in order to obtain the authentic Flying Tandoori flavors.

(Approx. 12–15 sausages)
1 lb (500 g) chicken meat (including skin), diced
1 lbs (500 g) turkey meat (including skin), diced
2 ½ tbsp tandoori paste
½ cup (100 ml) cilantro, finely chopped
2 tbsp honey
2 tbsp fish sauce
1 tsp chili flakes
1 ½ tsp non-iodized salt
½ cup (100 ml) coconut milk, ice cold

Grind the turkey and chicken meat on the coarsest setting. Mix the meat with the spices and coconut milk for about 5 minutes.
Fry a piece of the meat and sample.
Form the meat on skewers and refrigerate for 1–2 hours before cooking. Ideally, the skewers should be grilled—either in a pan or in the oven—but they are, of course, also delicious when fried.

SERVING

If you want the authentic Indian experience, the skewers should be served on a metal tray, but this is hardly essential. Simply place all the condiments in small bowls. Maybe you could swap this for weekly taco night? Yeah, make your dinners a little wild and crazy—Indian style!
Grill the skewers and serve with naan, tzatsiki, and different types of pickles and sauces for the ultimate experience!

NAAN

Can be bought at the store. Grill quickly before serving.

TZATZIKI

See the recipe for Greek Plate Down Under on page 123.

MANGO KETCHUP

See the recipe for Duck Duck on page 128.

PICKLES AND ROOT VEGETABLES

See the recipe for Knucklehead on page 47.

PICKLED CHILIES

See the recipe for Chili All In on page 43.

PICKLED GREEN TOMATOES

See the recipe for Southern Corn Dog on page 52.

AMERICAN BREAKFAST

CIDER CHICKEN AND HASH BROWNS WITH APPLE KETCHUP AND HORSERADISH

"A CHICKEN SAUSAGE WITH a hint of apple can never go wrong!" Johan thought to himself. And he was right. Apples and onions provide a perfect balance of flavors. The breadcrumbs are optional, but they make the sausage a little less firm and a little drier. If you can't find the Japanese breadcrumbs "panko," use regular bread with the crust cut off. The egg whites help bind the forcemeat, but they can also be omitted.

(Approx. 10–12 sausages)
3 apples, peeled and shredded
1 onion, finely chopped
2 lbs (1 kg) chicken meat (including skin), diced
¾ cup (200 ml) panko bread crumbs
2 egg whites
½ tsp dried salvia
2 tsp dried tarragon
1 tbsp dried parsley
2 tsp non-iodized salt
½ tsp freshly ground black pepper
½ cup (100 ml) dry apple cider, ice-cold

Fry the apples and onions in an oiled pan for 5–6 minutes while stirring constantly. When they become soft, remove from the stove and let cool. Grind the chicken meat on the coarsest setting.

Mix the meat with the apples, onions, breadcrumbs, egg whites, spices, and cider for 10 minutes. Fry a piece of the meat and sample.

Stuff the meat in pork casings and make sausages that are about 4 inches (10 cm) long.

Hang dry for 1–2 hours before refrigerating overnight. This will allow ample time for the flavors to develop.

Fry, grill, or cook the sausage before serving.

SERVING

This is simple and straightforward—it's an American breakfast! Fry or grill a couple of the sausages and serve with hash browns. Hash browns and their cousin, the potato pancake work very well as a side to delicious sausages. Mix the batter and fry in whatever portion size you like. Add ketchup and apple jam and top with fresh horseradish for an extra kick.

HASH BROWNS

4 mealy potatoes, peeled
1 onion, peeled
1 egg
salt and pepper

Shred the potatoes and onions and mix with the egg. Add salt and pepper to taste.

Fry portions of desired size in oil or butter until they turn golden.

APPLE KETCHUP WITH HORSERADISH

½ cup (100 ml) sugar
½ cup (100 ml) apple cider vinegar
1 shallot, finely chopped
¾ cup (200 ml) apple jam
½ of a red chili, diced
¼ cup (50 ml) freshly grated horseradish
salt

Melt the butter until it turns golden. Add the vinegar and chopped shallot.
Simmer until the sugar has dissolved.
Add the apple jam and chili and simmer until it becomes the desired consistency.
Remove from the stove and add the horseradish.
Add salt to taste.

TURKEY DOG IN A BASKET

JALAPEÑO TURKEY WITH HUSH PUPPIES, PICKLED WATERMELON, AND MUSTARD SLAW

THIS TURKEY DOG IS inspired by an American recipe and just has to be included. You'll go crazy for the fresh jalapeño chili! It's not too spicy, and it provides a clean, fresh flavor. You can lessen the spiciness by reducing the amount of chili used (but don't leave out the jalapeño!).

It's important to include the skin from the turkey in order to make the sausage juicy.

This sausage works best grilled and is perfect for whenever you crave a spicy turkey dog!

(Approx. 8–10 sausages)
2 lbs (1 kg) turkey meat (include the skin), diced
3 garlic cloves, finely chopped
2 jalapeño chilies, seeded and finely chopped
½ tbsp cumin
2 tsp chili powder
½ tsp chili flakes
1 tbsp non-iodized salt
½ tbsp coarsely ground black pepper
⅔ cup (150 ml) beer, ice-cold

Grind the turkey meat on the coarsest setting.

Mix forcemeat, spices, and beer for 10 minutes.

Fry a piece of the meat and sample.

Stuff the meat in pork casings and make sausages that are 8–10 inches (20–25 cm) long.

Hang dry for 1–2 hours before refrigerating overnight. This will allow the flavors ample time to develop. Fry, grill, or cook before serving.

SERVING

It's time for some finger food! Grab your food directly from the basket—like in a mid-west highway diner. (This is the perfect dish for a Route 66 themed party!)

Hush puppies are a traditional American side dish. Pickled watermelon is both delicious and fun. Remove the outer skin with a potato peeler and keep it for some extra crisp.

Remember: Budweiser has got to be served cold. Let's party!

HUSH PUPPIES

See the recipe for Blood Sausage in Madrid on page 59.

PICKLED WATERMELON

1 lb (500 g) watermelon rinds
    (1 x 1 inches [3 x 3 cm])
2 cups (500 ml) sugar
1 cup (250 ml) apple cider vine-
    gar
4–6 cloves
1 cinnamon stick
1 piece of ginger, sliced

Bring the water to a boil and let the watermelon cubes simmer until they soften (about 10 minutes). Place the watermelon cubes in jars. Bring the sugar, vinegar, cloves, cinnamon, and ginger to a boil. When the sugar has dissolved, pour the mixture over the watermelon, place a lid on top, and let the jars cool.

MUSTARD SLAW

See the recipe for Over-the-Top Bacon on page 80.

HALF A SPECIAL

**SMOKY MANGO DUCK IN A BUN WITH
MASHED POTATOES AND HONEY MUSTARD**

IF YOU HAVE ACCESS to a real meat smoker, you should use it for this sausage. Otherwise, simply add liquid smoke and dry the sausage in the oven. Make sure to rinse the sausages immediately in cold water when they're done. Ideally you should let them sit for 1–2 days in order to develop a smokier flavor. When it's time to eat, simply boil, fry, or grill!
This sausage is rather sweet due to the mango chutney. There are many different varieties of the chutney but here we're using the spicier kind. If you don't want to smoke the sausages, simply fry or grill them when they're done.

(Approx. 23–25)
1 ½ lbs (750 g) duck breast, with fat
½ lb (250 g) lard
4 tbsp smooth Bengal mango chutney
1 tsp garam masala
1 ½ tbsp liquid smoke
2 tsp non-iodized salt
1 tsp coarsely ground black pepper
⅔ cup (150 ml) heavy cream, ice-cold

Grind the duck meat on the finest setting.

Mix the forcemeat with the mango chutney, spices, and cream for about 10 minutes.

Fry a piece of the meat and sample.

Stuff the meat in sheep casings and make sausages that are 8–10 inches (20–25 cm) long.

Heat the oven to 170°F (75°C). Hang the sausages in the oven (make sure that they do not touch each other) and dry for 3 hours.

Remove and quickly rinse in cold water until they reach a temperature of 60°F (15°C).

Let them dry before storing in the refrigerator (ideally wrapped in parchment paper).

Fry, grill, or boil before serving.

SERVING

Hurrah for Gothenburg and its mashed potatoes! While we're at it, why not try a Whole Special? (For those of you not familiar with these terms, Half a Special = a hot dog with mashed potatoes, and a Whole Special = two dogs in a bun with mashed potatoes.)

Some homemade hot honey mustard will take this dish to the next level. You should eat this western Swedish dish without a fork—messy but delicious!

HOT DOG BUNS

See the recipe for Oh Deer! on page 108.

MASHED POTATOES
HOT HONEY MUSTARD

See the recipe for Knucklehead on page 47.

SALMON & SHRIMP MENU

SALMON AND SHRIMP WITH KIMCHI AIOLI, JALAPEÑO SLAW, AND DEEP-FRIED ONIONS

IT'S REALLY EASY TO make sausage out of salmon. Think "pâté" in a sausage shape. This particular sausage contains chopped shrimp for consistency and herbs for flavor.

Make sure that the sausage doesn't get too hot during the steaming process because that could cause the liquid to evaporate and dry the sausage out.

You can choose to serve it boiled, but it's best when browned in butter.

(Approx. 4–6 sausages)
1 ½ lbs (600 g) diced salmon
3 eggs
¾ cup (200 ml) sour cream
½ cup (50 g) Panko breadcrumbs
¼ cup (50 ml) chopped cilantro
¼ cup (50 ml) chopped parsley
½–1 chili, finely chopped
1 tsp salt
¼ tsp white pepper
½ lb (250 g) chopped shrimp

In a food processor, mix the salmon, egg, sour cream, breadcrumbs, herbs, and chili. Add salt and pepper to taste. Add the shrimp. Fry a piece of the mixture and sample.

Distribute the batter onto 4–6 pieces of plastic wrap and form sausages. Make sure the ends are properly sealed.

Steam the sausages at 195–210°F (90–100°C) so that the middle part reaches a temperature of 150°F (65°C). Remove from the steam and let them cool.

(Steam in a colander covered with a lid that has been placed over a saucepan filled with boiling water, or in the oven with a water basin under the oven rack.)

Remove the plastic wrap and fry the sausages in butter. Store in the refrigerator or the freezer.

SERVING

Serve the sausages after frying them in butter. Add some coleslaw made with jalapeño, Korean aioli flavored with kimchi paste, and deep-fried onions. (Fried onions go with any type of sausage!)

KIMCHI AIOLI

2 egg yolks
1 tbsp Dijon mustard
1–2 tbsp kimchi paste
1 tbsp lemon juice
1–2 tbsp rapeseed oil
salt and white pepper

Place the egg yolks, mustard, lemon juice, and kimchi paste in a bowl and whisk. Gradually add the oil while stirring.

Add salt, pepper, and possibly some extra kimchi paste and lemon juice to taste.

(You can purchase kimchi paste in any Asian grocery store.)

JALAPEÑO SLAW

2 lbs (1 kg) cabbage
1–2 carrots, shredded
1 jalapeño chili, thinly sliced
¾ cup (200 ml) mayonnaise
1 tbsp lemon juice
2 tbsp rapeseed oil
2 tbsp sugar
½ tsp celery salt
salt and pepper

Start by cutting the cabbage into thin shreds.
Bring some lightly salted water to a boil and
add the cabbage. Boil for about 2–3 minutes.
Drain the water and let the cabbage rinse off.
Squeeze out the last of the water with your
hands.
Place the cabbage in a bowl along with the car-
rots and sliced jalapeños.
In a separate bowl, add the mayonnaise, lemon
juice, oil, sugar, and celery salt. Add salt and pepper to taste.
Mix the contents of the bowls. Let sit for 30–40 minutes before serving.

DEEP-FRIED ONIONS

See the recipe for Chili All In on page 43.

MOULES DE MER

CRAB AND LOBSTER SAUSAGE WITH MOULES MARINIÈRE AND FRENCH FRIES

WATCH OUT, IT'S TIME for some luxury—west coast style! This sumptuous sausage should be stuffed in sheep casings for best results. You can also roll them in plastic foil and steam them, but they won't have the same finish.

(For more information on how to steam fish sausage, see the recipe for Salmon & Shrimp Menu on page 144.)

Let's say this is a "Surf and Surf." For best results, make sure the crabmeat is evenly distributed. It shouldn't be mixed or ground because that will destroy the nice seafood consistency. The lobster is added as is, with both tail and claws. The egg yolks and breadcrumbs are what bind the meat together, so make sure you have a firm batter. (The seasoning may vary, but if it's too hot it may cancel out the taste of the seafood.)

(Approx. 28–30 sausages)

¾ lb (350 g) crabmeat (from the claw)

⅓ lb (150 g) lobster meat, diced as small as possible (¼ inch x ¼ inch [½ x ½ cm])

2 egg yolks

½ cup (100 ml) mayonnaise

½ cup (100 ml) panko breadcrumbs

2 shallots, sliced

2 garlic cloves, chopped

½ cup (100 ml) chopped parsley

2 tbsp olive oil

1 tsp Colman's mustard powder

½ tsp cayenne pepper

1 tsp salt

¼ tsp freshly ground white pepper

Mix the crab and the lobster meat. Stir in the rest of the ingredients and add salt and pepper to taste.

Fry a piece of the mixture and sample.

Stuff the meat in sheep casings and make sausages that are 2–3 inches (5–7 cm) long.

Poach the sausages in water at a temperature of 175–195°F (80–90°C) until the middle part is 140°F (60°C).

Remove and rinse the sausages in cold water until they reach a temperature of 60°F (15°C). Store in the refrigerator. Boil, fry, or grill the sausages before serving.

SERVING

The poached sausages taste phenomenal when added to Moules Marinière. Either boil, fry, or grill according to the recipe above, or you can add them straight to the soup and let them finish cooking there.

Serve with Belgian style fries.

MOULES MARINIÈRE

1 bag of mussels, cleaned
2 tbsp butter
1 onion, chopped
2 garlic cloves, chopped
1 carrot, chopped
1 celery stalk, chopped
5 sprigs of thyme
2–3 sprigs of parsley
¾ cup (200 ml) white wine
¾ cup (200 ml) heavy cream
salt and white pepper

Melt the butter in a saucepan and sweat the onions, garlic, carrots, and celery for a couple of minutes.

Add the mussels, thyme, parsley, and wine. Cover with a lid.

Bring the mixture to a boil and make sure the mussels open. (Throw away any that don't open!)

Add the cream and bring to a boil. Add salt and pepper to taste.

When serving, bring the mussels to a boil again and serve immediately.

FRENCH FRIES

See the recipe for Homage to Konnopke on page 70.

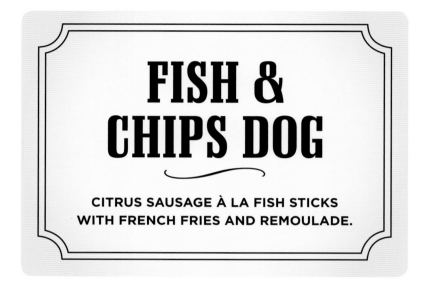

FISH & CHIPS DOG

CITRUS SAUSAGE À LA FISH STICKS
WITH FRENCH FRIES AND REMOULADE.

FISH AND CHIPS ARE a pub favorite not only in Britain but also in Sweden and America. This is the homemade version—the best kind! Nothing beats freshly cut, homemade French fries and remoulade. Use the catch of the day from the pier, boat, or fish counter. We won't stuff the meat into casings. Rather, we'll double bread the fish meat. Form to the desired size, and then roll in flour, beaten egg, and breadcrumbs (in this case, we're using the Japanese version called panko).

(Approx. 8–10 sausages)
1 lb (500 g) white fish (e.g. pollock, cod, or haddock)
1 egg
½ cup (100 ml) chopped parsley
1 lemon peel
2 tsp chili flakes
1 tsp salt
¼ tsp cayenne pepper
¾ cup (200 ml) flour
2 eggs, beaten
¾–1 ¼ cups (200–300 ml) panko breadcrumbs
deep-frying oil

Grind half of the fish on the coarsest setting. Dice the rest of the fish into cubes of roughly half an inch square (1 x 1 cm).

Mix the ground meat with the fish cubes and egg. Add the parsley and lemon zest.

Season with chili flakes, salt, and cayenne pepper.

Fry a piece of the meat and sample.

Roll the meat and cut into 4 inch (10 cm) long sausages. Roll them first in flour, then the beaten egg, and lastly in the panko.

Heat a fryer and oil to 340–355°F (170–180°C) and fry the sausages for 4–5 minutes until they turn a nice golden color.

If you choose not to fry them all at once, the remaining sausages should be stored in the refrigerator or freezer. Simply toss them in the fryer before serving.

If you don't wish to deep-fry the sausages, you may also fry them in a pan with a generous amount of oil.

SERVING

A Fish and Chips Dog requires French fries. These are fried a few at a time and are simply first rate—world class! And we will, of course, add remoulade. Don't make the remoulade too smooth, though. Aim for a more "homemade" consistency!

FRENCH FRIES

See the recipe for Homage to Konnopke on page 70.

REMOULADE

1 ½ cups (250 g) pickles
½ cup (100 ml) mayonnaise
¼ cup (50 ml) sour cream
2 tbsp Dijon mustard
1 tbsp curry
½ tsp cayenne pepper
1 tsp cumin
½ tsp Tabasco
salt and black pepper

Mix the pickles in a blender, then add the rest of the ingredients. Season with Tabasco, salt, and pepper to taste. As mentioned earlier, make sure it's not too smooth!

FLATBREAD WITH EXTRA EVERYTHING

SCALLOP SAUSAGE WITH MASHED POTATOES, SHRIMP SALAD, BLEAK ROE, AND DEEP-FRIED ONIONS

A SAUSAGE WITH SCALLOPS! In a flatbread! This right here is fine dining meets street food. It makes for the best sandwich!

This exclusive sausage will impress friends and guests, and it's not very hard to prepare. It's rolled in plastic wrap, not casings. So simple, so delicious!

Aside from scallops, the forcemeat contains a bit of neutral white fish. But this isn't necessary if you're going to go "all in" with the scallops.

Feel free to keep some scallop chunks in the sausage—it adds to the consistency. This sausage should be steamed first so that it holds together better when fried.

(Approx. 8–10 sausages)
1 lb (500 g) scallops, de-frosted and split
½ lb (200 g) diced white fish (e.g. pollock, cod, or haddock)
2 egg whites
½ cup (100 ml) heavy cream
½ of a chili, diced
1 garlic clove, pressed
½ cup (100 ml) chopped chives
1 tsp salt
¼ tsp white pepper

Mix the fish and two thirds of a pound of the scallops with the egg whites and cream.

Dice the rest of the scallops into cubes roughly half an inch square [1 x 1 cm] and mix with the chili, garlic, and chives. Add salt and pepper to taste.

Fry a piece of the meat and sample (try not to eat it all!). Distribute onto plastic wrap and roll firm sausages that are 8–10 inches (20–25 cm) long. Steam the sausages at 195–210°F (90–100°C) until the centers reach 140°F (60°C). Remove and let them cool.

(For more information about steaming fish sausage, see the recipe for Salmon & Shrimp Menu on page 144.)

Remove the plastic wrap and fry in butter before serving.

SERVING

"What can I say? All of the fuses blew and this is the result! The best flat-bread sandwich with extra everything!" said Johan. If you want to enjoy the most delicious flatbread sandwich, do as he says!

Spread butter onto a flatbread and add mashed potatoes containing butter and cream, some slices of fried scallop sausages, a fair amount of shrimp salad, topped with bleak roe caviar, and fried onions. You can also choose to add some of the cocktail ketchup from page 51. Roll up and enjoy!

MASHED POTATOES

See the recipe for Knucklehead on page 47.

SHRIMP SALAD

⅔ lb (300 g) shrimp, peeled and drained
¼ lb (100 g) white radishes, diced and
  poached
½ cup (100 ml) mayonnaise
¼ cup (50 ml) sour cream
2 tbsp ketchup
½ tbsp Dijon mustard
½ tsp Tabasco
½ tbsp lemon juice
salt and pepper

Combine the shrimp and white radishes with the mayonnaise, sour cream, ketchup, and Dijon mustard. Add Tabasco, lemon juice, salt and pepper to taste.

DEEP-FRIED ONIONS

See the recipe for Chili All In on page 43.

DEEP-FRIED SPRING ROLL SAUSAGE

TOM YAM SAUSAGE IN SPRING ROLL BATTER WITH KIMCHI, DIPPING SAUCE, AND PICKLED CHILIES.

A SAUSAGE NEEDS TO have a "skin," no? Well, in this recipe, the meat is rolled in spring roll batter. Spring rolls? Isn't this a sausage cookbook? Yes, but both the sausage and this roll have two ends.

So no quibbling—let's go!

You can make this sausage the traditional way as is described in some of the other recipes: i.e. stuffed in casings, breaded, rolled in plastic wrap, or simply formed with your hands.

The Thai soup Tom Yam is the source of inspiration. "I just tried to squeeze all the flavors into the sausage, and I think I succeeded pretty well!" says Johan.

(Approx. 8–10 sausages)
1 tbsp sesame oil
1 onion, diced
2 garlic cloves, chopped
10 mushrooms, sliced
1 chili pepper, sliced
1 lb (500 g) giant shrimp, diced
1 lb (500 g) white fish, diced
½ cup (100 ml) finely chopped cilantro
2 tbsp Tom Yam paste
1 tbsp fish sauce

1 tbsp lime juice
1 tbsp black sesame seeds
1 tbsp honey
1 egg
1 tsp salt
½ cup (100 ml) coconut milk, ice-cold
8–10 pieces of spring roll wrapper (11 x 11 inches [30 x 30 cm])
flour for sealing
deep-frying oil

Fry the onions, mushroom, and chilies in the sesame oil. Grind the giant shrimp, fish, and mushroom mix on the coarsest setting. Stir in the rest of the ingredients and the coconut milk and mix for 5 minutes. Fry a piece of the meat and sample.

Distribute the meat onto the wrappers and roll into sausages that are 8–10 inches (20–25 cm) long. Seal with a mixture of flour and water.

Heat the oil in the deep fryer to 340–355°F (170–180°C) and deep-fry the sausages until they turn golden and float to the surface (about 4–5 minutes).

Store in the freezer. Toss in the fryer before serving.

SERVING

This sausage is fried and served with kimchi—a Korean version of sauerkraut—some good Vietnamese dipping sauce, and pickled chilies for extra heat.

QUICK KIMCHI

1 head of bok choi
4 sliced shallots
¼ cup (50 ml) kimchi paste
1–2 tbsp fish sauce
salt

Mix salt and some water and add the sliced cabbage. Let sit for an hour. Remove the water and quickly wash the cabbage. Rinse it off.

Mix the cabbage , shallots, and kimchi paste, and add fish sauce and salt to taste

Let sit for an hour or two before serving.

Kimchi paste can be purchased in any Asian grocery store.

NUOC CHAM (VIETNAMESE DIPPING SAUCE)

See the recipe for Banh Mi Total on page 62.

PICKLED CHILIES

See the recipe for Chili All In on page 43.

M. CHORIZO M. BAMSE   30

CHORIZO M BRÖD   25

BAMSE M. BRÖD   25

LAMMKORV M BRÖD   3

KALL DRYCK 10:-

VEGETARIAN

SMOKED VEGETARIAN SAUSAGE

SMOKY BEAN SAUSAGE IN PITA BREAD WITH SALAD, PICKLES, AND KETCHUP

IF YOU'RE CRAVING SMOKED sausage but don't eat meat, this will be your salvation.

The main ingredients are kidney beans and corn, and the seasoning consists of garlic, fennel, chili, paprika, and oregano.

The smoky flavor comes from the liquid smoke.

Let the batter sit and "mature" when it is mixed in order to give the sausage more flavor.

No casings needed—simply roll the sausages in plastic wrap and steam.

Fry the sausages before serving.

(Approx. 6–8 sausages)
1 ¼ cups (300 ml) kidney beans, cooked
1 cup (250 ml) corn
1 onion, diced
2 garlic cloves
½ cup (100 ml) parsley
⅔ cup (150 ml) cornmeal
1 egg white

1 tbsp olive oil
2 tbsp Japanese soy sauce
1 tbsp liquid smoke
1 ½ tsp crushed fennel seeds
1 tsp chili flakes
1 tsp hot paprika
1 tsp dried oregano
1 ½ tsp salt
1 tsp freshly ground black pepper

Grind the beans, three-fourths of a cup of corn, onion, garlic, and parsley on the coarsest setting.

Mix with the other ingredients and let sit at room temperature for 3–4 hours.

Fry a piece of the batter and sample.

Distribute the batter onto 6–8 pieces of plastic wrap and make sausages that are 8–10 inches (20–25 cm) long.

Steam the sausages for 20 minutes, then let them cool.

(For more information on how to steam sausage, see the recipe for Salmon & Shrimp Menu on page 144.)

Remove the plastic wrap and fry the sausages in oil until they turn golden.

SERVING

"Handmad" say the Danish. The rest of us call it simple and delicious "street food!"

Either way, sausage served in pita bread is both practical and delicious, and it tastes amazing with some delicious condiments. Try to find large pita bread that is reminiscent of flatbread (which would work just as well). Add whatever you like.

This recipe suggests lettuce, pickles with chili, and ketchup with apple and horseradish.

PICKLED CUCUMBER WITH CHILI

See the recipe for Wallenberger on page 93.

APPLE KETCHUP WITH HORSERADISH

See the recipe for American Breakfast on page 135.

ASIAN DUMPLING MEAL

MUSHROOM AND RICE SAUSAGE IN A LETTUCE WRAP WITH VIETNAMESE DIPPING SAUCE AND PICKLED ROOT VEGETABLES.

"WHEN I WAS IN Vietnam, I had the most delicious dumplings filled with exciting meats and flavors. I had the thought of making sausages out of them and serving them like that," says Johan.

Be sure to mix the flour before adding the water which should be about 176°F (80°C) for best results. Use a ladle to avoid getting burned! Mix the dough and knead in the mushroom mix.

Form the sausages and poach them in salted water until they rise to the surface. You can also boil or fry them.

(For more information about the Asian ingredients in this recipe, see the section Nice 2 Know on page 184.)

(Approx. 25–30 sausages)
⅓ lb (150 g) mushrooms
2 shallots, chopped
2 garlic cloves, chopped
2 tbsp rapeseed oil
2 tbsp chili bean paste
¾ cup (200 ml) rice flour
¾ cup (200 ml) tapioca flour
2 tbsp sticky rice flour
⅔ cup (150 ml) water (176°F [80°C])
1 tsp salt
¼ cup (50 ml) rapeseed oil
½ cup (100 ml) roasted onion

Heat the oil in a pan and fry the mushrooms, onions, and garlic. Add chili bean paste and salt to taste and set aside to cool.

In a large bowl, mix all the different flours and make a dent in the middle. Gradually add the water while stirring and knead until it becomes a dough. Add the mushroom mixture. Form sausages that are about 4 inches (10 cm) long.

Bring salted water to a boil and add 5–7 sausages at a time. Let simmer until they float to the surface. Remove and roll the sausages in some oil and roasted onions. Serve immediately.

SERVING

The dumpling fad is here! Soon there is likely to be a dumpling place at every corner.

However, you don't have to buy them at restaurants—you can make dumpling sausage instead!

Serve the "sausages" freshly cooked. Roll in oil, then in roasted onions. Ideally, wrap a piece of lettuce around the sausage and add some root vegetables. Then just dip them in sauce and enjoy!

NUOC CHAM (VIETNAMESE DIPPING SAUCE)

See the recipe for Banh Mi Total on page 62.

PICKLED ROOT VEGETABLES

See the recipe for Knucklehead on page 47.

VEGGIE WURST IN A BUN

DEEP-FRIED CHICKPEA AND CHILI WURST IN A BUN WITH BOSTON RELISH

THIS IS ALMOST A falafel, but oblong. You can choose to follow this recipe or purchase falafel mix instead. However, this chickpea and chili wurst is much more delicious because it's spiked with chili, cilantro, and parsley.

Make oblong "sausages" so that they fit in a bun. Make sure to deep-fry them a little extra so that they stay together in the bread. You can, of course, choose to make small little balls as well. It's important to let the batter rise for a while before deep-frying. You can also fry the sausages/balls in a pan with a generous amount of oil.

(Approx. 14–15 sausages)
2 tbsp olive oil
2 onions, chopped
2 garlic cloves, chopped
1 tsp ground cumin
2 tsp ground cilantro
4 cups (800 g) cooked chickpeas
1 cup (250 ml) chopped parsley
1–2 green chili peppers, seeded and finely chopped
⅔ cup (150 ml) flour
1 egg white
2 tsp salt
deep-frying oil

Heat the olive oil in a pan and sweat the onion, garlic, cumin, and cilantro until the onions turn golden. Set aside and let cool.

Grind the chickpeas, onion mixture, and parsley on the finest setting. Or run it through a mixer.

Mix with chili, flour, egg white, and salt. Let rise for 30 minutes.

Heat the oil to 340–355°F (170–180°C) and use a piping bag to pipe out a couple of dollops into the fryer at a time.

Deep-fry for 4–5 minutes or until they turn golden. Remove and serve.

SERVING

This vegetarian wurst should be served like a regular hot dog with Boston relish. This is made from regular pickles but you can also find the specific recipe for "Boston pickles" and customize it even more!

HOT DOG BUNS

See the recipe for Oh Deer! on page 108.

BOSTON RELISH

⅔ cup (300 g) drained pickles
½ cup (100 ml) ajvar relish
Tabasco
salt

Place the pickles in a blender and mix.

Add the ajvar relish. Season with Tabasco and salt to taste.

TOFU & CHIPS

DEEP-FRIED, SPICY TOFU ROLL WITH FRENCH FRIES AND CHILI KETCHUP

TOFU IS DELICIOUS, VARIED, and healthy. In order to make the sausage stick together and provide some chewy resistance, it's important to squeeze as much water as possible from the tofu. This sausage uses phyllo as a casing. You can also use plastic wrap and steam, freeze, and re-fry them. The benefit of the phyllo is that it provides a crispy surface. The seasoning is delicious and is just a bit on the hot side. Ideally you should let it sit and "mature" before serving.

(Approx. 6–8 sausages)
¾ lb (400 g) tofu, sliced
1 tbsp ground ancho chili
4 garlic cloves, pressed
1 tbsp oregano
2 tsp paprika
1 ½ tsp cumin
1 tsp salt
½ tsp chili flakes
½ tsp ground cloves
½ tsp ground cinnamon
2 tbsp apple cider vinegar
¼ cup (50 ml) peanut butter
¾ cup (200 ml) rapeseed oil
6–8 sheets of phyllo

Grab a kitchen towel and place the pieces of tofu in the center. Cover with the towel and let sit under pressure for one hour in order to squeeze out the liquids.

Place all of the other ingredients (except the rapeseed oil and phyllo) in a blender and mix until it becomes smooth.

Add the tofu and mix again.

Distribute the batter on sheets of phyllo. Brush with the oil and make sausages that are about 12 inches (30 cm) long. The ends should emulate a British Christmas cracker.

Keep them under plastic wrap until they are ready to be cooked.

The sausages should be fried, cooked in the oven for 10 minutes at a temperature of 390°F (200°C) (brushed with oil), or deep-fried.

SERVING

Sausage served with French fries and ketchup can never go wrong and this recipe is particularly fantastic! If you choose to deep-fry this tofu chorizo, you should do it at the same time as you are deep-frying the French fries. Take the time to cook in rounds—it's well worth the trouble. Garnish with the chili ketchup for an extra kick.

FRENCH FRIES

See the recipe for Homage to Konnopke on page 70.

CHILI KETCHUP

See the recipe for Blood Sausage in Madrid on page 59.

THE DESIGNER

ZUCCHINI AND MOZZARELLA ROLL WITH HOT SALSA AND FRIED ONION RINGS

WHY IS THIS BANGIN' recipe in the back of the book? Let's just say that it's incredibly delicious and super simple to cook. All you have to do is cook it, mix, roll in breadcrumbs, deep-fry or fry, and enjoy. Not a single casing in sight! A great way to wrap up the book and get you making sausage!

This recipe contains mozzarella, which can be switched out for any other cheese according to preference.

It's important to squeeze as much liquid from the zucchini as possible before making the batter. The bread will make the sausage "airy" and juicy, and instead of casings, we'll roll the sausage in breadcrumbs before deep-frying or pan frying.

You can easily transform this batter into patties as well.

The sausage gets its name from this book's vegetarian designer, Pär. With a professional enthusiasm, he devoted himself to all of the sausages in this book, including the ones containing meat. In the end, we dedicated an entire vegetarian recipe to him, and it instantly became one of his favorites. Give "The Designer" a try!

(Approx. 8–10 sausages)
½ lb (175 g) toast
1 zucchini, shredded
2 tbsp (25 g) butter
1 onion, chopped
1 ½ cups (150 g) grated mozzarella
½ cup (100 ml) chopped kalamata olives (remove the seeds)
1 egg (divided)
1 tsp salt
½ tsp freshly ground black pepper

Place the bread in a blender and mix until it becomes breadcrumbs.

Salt the zucchini and let sit for 10 minutes. Then, squeeze out as much liquid as possible.

Fry the onions in butter until they turn golden. Add the zucchini and fry it together with the onions for another 3–4 minutes before letting the mixture cool.

Mix the zucchini and the onions with half of the breadcrumbs and the mozzarella, olives, and egg yolks. Add salt and pepper to taste.

Form sausages that are 3–4 inches (8–10 cm) long. Roll them in the beaten egg whites and then in the remaining breadcrumbs.

Fry in a generous amount of oil (or deep-fry) before serving.

SERVING

These wonderfully easy sausage rolls should be fried in a generous amount of oil. Just make sure that the heat isn't set too high since that might overcook or burn them. As an alternative, you can deep-fry them. The choice is yours!

Serve with some crispy salsa and onion rings.

"This turned out delicious!" Johan proclaimed.

QUICK SALSA

See the recipe for Barbecue Sandwich with a Kick on page 29.

ONION RINGS

See the recipe for Mallorca in My Mouth on page 83.

— INDEX —

— NICE 2 KNOW —

GENERAL
The Sausage Academy was founded in 1991 and has 12 members, including Christina Möller, the previous CEO of KF/COOP test kitchen. She says, "I want to be the knight of sausages!" Other members include star chef Roland Persson, Ulf Elfving, Bo Hagström, and sausage enthusiast Jan Scherman.
The Academy organizes a tournament to determine Sausage Master of the Year, National Sausage Day at the Nordic Museum and the Royal Gardens in Stockholm, seminars, and exhibits. For more information, see its website: www.korvakademien.nu.

Swedish Prime Minister **Fredrik Reinfeldt** loves sausage. This fact was well established in an interview with David Hellenius on TV4. For more information about Fredrik's love for sausage and recipes, see www.fredrikskorvkasse.se.

When the world famous chef **Anthony Bourdain** was in Stockholm to promote his latest cookbook, his best culinary experience was a grilled hot dog with a shrimp salad. "I've never tasted anything like this! So good!"

Delicious, artisan sausages can be purchased at various **deli counters** and **farmer's markets**. Any American farmer's market ought to have a great assortment of international sausages with exotic flavors. You can also purchase them directly from farmers.

BASIC RECIPE
1½ lbs (800 g) diced meat
½ lb (200 g) lard
2–3 tsp salt
1 tsp pepper
1–3 tbsp spices
½ cup (100 ml) ice water or other
   liquid

Grind the meat and fat. Mix with the spices and liquids and stuff in casings.

Form sausages to desired size.
Hang until the surface dries.
Place in a bowl and refrigerate overnight so the flavors have ample time to develop.
Fry, grill, cook, or freeze.

COMMANDMENTS AND TECHNIQUE
* Keep it cold!
* Keep it clean!

These are the two most important rules of sausage making and when handling the ingredients. They are particularly important when making large batches, when the sausage is left lying around for longer. Make sure that all aspects of the cooking process are prepared beforehand (from the meat to the grinding, mixing, and stuffing). Wash your hands thoroughly throughout the process or use plastic gloves. Make sure the meat is as fresh as possible. Feel free to freeze the meat before using it because that reduces the meat temperature throughout the cooking process. When mixing, first add the fresh and wet ingredients, then the dry spices, and lastly the liquids. Ideally, you should mix the spices with a liquid beforehand so that they distribute more evenly through the meat.

SAUSAGE ONLINE
Inspiration
thespicysausage.com
www.salsus.se
www.lets-make-sausage.com
www.sausagemaking.org
www.sausagemania.com/index.html
www.wannerdt.com/jan-erik/korvar/
   mina_basta_korvrecept.shtml
www.alltomkorv.se
www.korvhuset.com

Equipment
http://www.sausagemaker.com/
http://www.westonsupply.com/Sausage-Making-s/71.htm
http://www.alliedkenco.com/
http://www.waltonsinc.com/

FURTHER READING

The Sausage Cookbook Bible
  by Ellen Brown
Hot Links and Country Flavors: Sausages in American Regional Cooking
  by Bruce Aidell
Great Sausage Recipes and Meat Curing
  by Rytek Kutas
The Art of Making Fermented Sausages
  by Adam Marianski
Charcuterie: The Craft of Salting, Smoking, and Curing
  by Brian Polcyn
Sausage: Recipes for Making and Cooking with Homemade Sausage
  by Victoria Wise
Sausage: A Country-by-Country Photographic Guide with Recipes
  by Nicola Fletcher

INGREDIENTS

Chili bean paste, tapioca flour, sticky rice flour, kimchi paste, and sriracha sauce can be found in Asian grocery stores.

Pimentón de la Vera is a Spanish smoky paprika and exists in two versions: dulce (sweet) and picante (hot). It can be found in grocery stores with wide selections or shops with an "exotic" section.

Casings/skins exist in numerous versions: from animals (e.g. pork, sheep, beef), plastic wrap, leaves (e.g. banana leaf), aluminum foil, sausages without "skin," artificial skins (collagen). These keep the meat together so that you can form the sausage into desired shapes.

You can find casings/skins in the deli section of the grocery store, at farmers markets, at the butcher shop, or online. See the attached links.

AUTHORS/CREATORS
Johan Åkerberg
Chef and gastronome inspired by the world. Runs the consulting firm Måltid in Stockholm. Provides culinary experiences in accordance with the motto: "Too much of the best is just enough!"

Jesper Lindberg
Musician, writer, and ex-cookbook publisher. His favorites: Habanero heat and a 5 string banjo in G major.

Pepe Nilsson
Photographer and globetrotter. He feels just as at home in Athens, Nice, and the Greek Islands as in the Stockholm archipelago and the photo studio on Kungsholmen. Inspired by the best in life!

Pär Wickholm
A designer and photographer of album covers and books. Has not eaten meat since the 1980s when he also wrote hateful punk songs about carnivores. Today he has a more nuanced understanding of healthy food culture.

EQUIPMENT
The simple way—economy class
* Readymade ground meat
* Measurements
* A mixing bowl
* Forcing bag for stuffing the sausage

The advanced way—business class
* Meat grinder
* Spice grinder
* Scale
* KitchenAid mixer
* Automatic Stuffing Machine
* Digital Thermometer
* Hooks

For the sausage enthusiast, there's an incredible assortment of sausage making equipment. You can be as advanced as you want, by purchasing drying cabinets, special refrigerators with humidity settings, pH and humidity meters, meat smokers, etc.

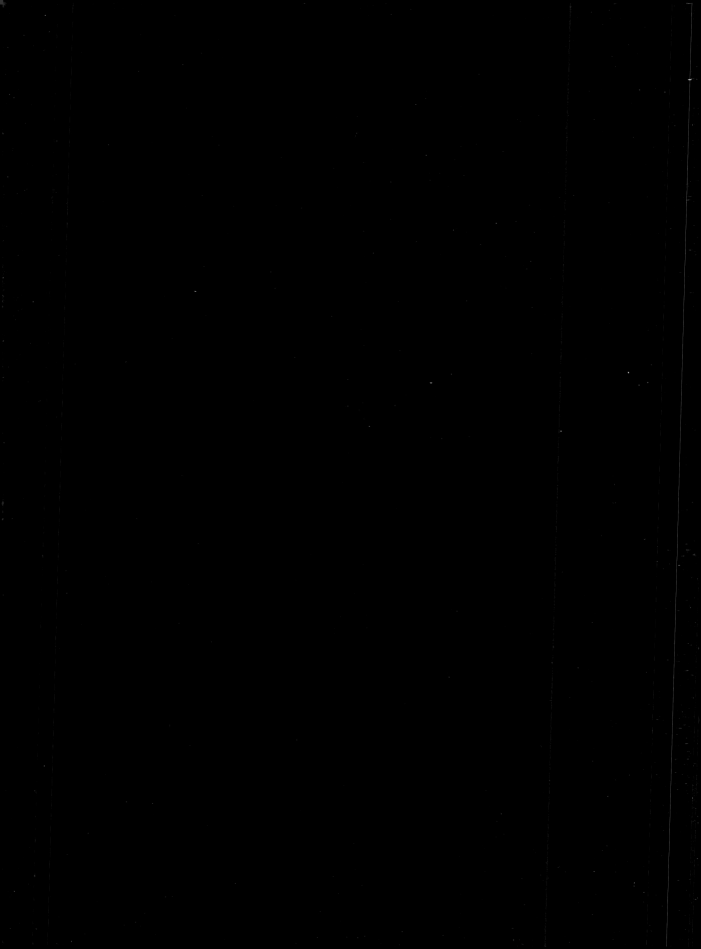